The Netherlands

KT-504-395

A guide to recent architecture

Kathy Battista and Florian Migsch
Photographs by Anna Neumann and Florian Migsch

The Netherlands

A guide to recent architecture

● ● ● **ellipsis** KÖNEMANN

•••

All rights reserved. No part of this publication may be reproduced in any form without written permission from the publisher

The Netherlands: a guide to recent architecture

PUBLISHED BY
Ellipsis London Limited
2 Rufus Street London N1 6PE
E MAIL ...@ellipsis.co.uk
www http://www.ellipsis.com
SERIES EDITOR Tom Neville
EDITOR Cristiano Ratti
SERIES DESIGN Jonathan Moberly
LAYOUT Pauline Harrison

  Nederlandse Spoorwegen

COPYRIGHT © 1998 Könemann
Verlagsgesellschaft mbH
Bonner Str. 126, D-50968 Köln
PRODUCTION MANAGER Detlev Schaper
PRINTING AND BINDING Sing Cheong
Printing Ltd
Printed in Hong Kong

ISBN 3 8290 0475 3 (Könemann)
ISBN 1 899858 57 1 (Ellipsis)

Kathy Battista and Florian Migsch 1998

Contents

Introduction	6
Using this book	13
Amsterdam	15
Noord Holland	71
Groningen and Friesland	95
Overijssel	131
Gelderland	139
Utrecht	153
Noord Brabant and Zeeland	189
Limburg	209
Rotterdam	235
Zuid Holland	283
Index	321

Introduction

This guide is not a comprehensive account of contemporary architecture in The Netherlands – several volumes would be necessary to cover the incredible range of work being done in the country. Rather, the book is a personal and subjective selection of the projects that are thought best to exemplify the spirit of Dutch architecture today. Sites were chosen not only for their physical merits, but also for the size and cost of the development, as well as the impact the building had on its location. Diversity was the main goal, and the building types span from toy containers on a human scale to large-scale housing and urban developments. A wide spread of practices are highlighted: more established firms may have some of their overall corpus represented, while younger offices, such as MVRDV and Neutelings Riedijk, almost have their entire œuvre here.

We worked on the project as 'inspired outsiders': neither of us had ever lived or worked in The Netherlands, and one of us is not an architect. The chance to research a topic such as this was exciting and our strategy was to see as much as possible and to talk to as many people involved with the making of buildings. We are not attempting to write a theoretical or in-depth analysis of Dutch architecture. This may be left to the writers at *Archis* and *De Architect*, whose expert opinions helped us to navigate a way through a large field of work. The more personal style of our guide is not meant to be irreverent. Rather we want to help engage a visitor to The Netherlands and provide the necessary facts about the building. The quotes that you will encounter are from architects, project managers, city planners and, at times, people using the building, such as museum directors. The openness of the Dutch and their willingness to cooperate never ceased to amaze and it is hoped that the anecdotes will allow the Dutch a voice in what is, essentially, their book.

Perhaps one of the reasons why we were so warmly greeted by the

Dutch is their attitude toward the new. From the beginning they have had to fight the encroaching sea. The need to renew and update the infrastructure has always been a cultural imperative: if the dykes were not repaired, the land would be flooded. That intrinsic discipline pervades all walks of life and there are beautiful examples of these collective endeavours; the impressive Delta Works in the Oosterschelde or the Polders on the IJsselmeer are examples of Dutch determination, foresight and engineering prowess. Huge tracts of land were reclaimed from the sea by building a barricade, draining the water, filling the infill and waiting years for the ground to be prepared. In the 1950s and 1960s urban planners of the modern movement designed entire towns on the new land almost as if they were playing with toy bricks. Unfortunately the planners often failed to fulfil the rosy expectations that initiated the town's construction.

Born of dire need, architecture has always been embraced by the Dutch on a social as well a cultural basis. The Housing Act of 1901 laid the foundation of a tradition for the provision of public housing. The legislation provided subsidies to pay for the difference between the cost and rent of the dwellings. Since then the construction of houses and subsequently town planning have become the declared policy of successive governments. The subsidies are dedicated to housing corporations, but do not exceed more than 8 per cent of the total budget. Another way for the municipalities to construct affordable housing was not to sell the plot but to lease it out for 50 years if the cooperative would construct apartments for use in the social sector. An essentially long-term policy, it is far more efficient than the passive systems of financing found in other European countries.

In 1995 the housing subsidies were withdrawn because the government wanted the private sector to be more involved. The sudden change in financing has turned housing corporations from stable market forces that would guarantee a quality of production to development agencies. It is perhaps fitting that *opdrachgever* describes a far more complex relationship than the English equivalent, 'client'.

The intertwined roles of architects and politicians have deeply affected the urban culture of Dutch cities. The architectural quality of a town can often be linked with the sophistication of their Alderman. Adri Duivesteijn of The Hague became prominent for the role he played during the competition for the City Hall. He by-passed OMA's winning entry and replaced it with a project by American architect Richard Meier, a political decision that literally split the municipality in half. Nevertheless, Duivesteijn made a career of his affection for architecture: following the coup to install Meier's design, he became the first director of The Netherlands Architecture Institute in Rotterdam.

In Amersfoort, Ben van Berkel and Caroline Bos could not have built an internationally recognised body of work without the continuing support of Alderman Frans Asselberg. The architectural talent he attracted for the city's extensions gave an identity to the suburbs. In terms of urban planning, Riek Bakker is one of the key players in the country. She was the administrator who had the political farsightedness to bring the immense Kop van Zuid extension in Rotterdam to fruition. Thereafter her move to the national stage meant becoming involved with 'The Hague New City Centre' and the western extension of Utrecht in the Leidse Rijn.

Political involvement in the housing programmes and the resulting stability are one side of the Dutch success story. The necessary financial resources are provided by huge investment funds controlled by the Dutch banking system. Rem Koolhaas ridiculed the consortia once by remarking that, although provincial, they 'own half of Manhattan'. The return from their global interests is invested in housing. Governmental programmes such as the current VINEX (an abbreviation for the Fourth Extra Spatial Policy) would not be possible without investment from the financial sector. VINEX, which will provide 800,000 dwelling units by 2005, is entirely financed by developers who are at the bottom end of the chain owned by the five biggest Dutch banks. The sheer scale of this kind of investment does not happen anywhere else in Europe.

The Dutch attitude towards the new is reflected today in the tremendous amount of building taking place. Schemes such as De Resident in The Hague involve a total renovation of the inner city as well as the co-operation of private and civic authorities. Museums are expanding or building new premises, and there is a need for the huge quantity of housing over the next decade. While the country is not yet overpopulated, there is not too much land available.

The implied efficiency of any new urban quarter is always linked to the infrastructure available. City centres are invigorated by large interventions such as the Erasmus Bridge in Rotterdam or the network of underground carparks currently under construction in The Hague. Sometimes these services gain national notoriety, as the discussions about the terrace of the high speed train, HSL, illustrate. The urgency to realise the architectural potential of the ever-growing infrastructure has been thematised in the first place by the Office for Metropolitan Architecture (OMA) in Rotterdam.

The legacy of OMA is seen today in the trickle-down effect. The pervasive presence of its principal, Rem Koolhaas, is felt worldwide. The 'Documenta' exhibition, held every 5 years in Kassel, Germany, in 1997 included for the first time in many years a cross-section of architectural designs. Among the offices and artists on display were Koolhaas and Aldo van Eyck, himself a veteran of Dutch structuralism. We spoke to the critic Joost Meuwissen about Koolhaas' influence on Dutch architects:

Joost Meuwissen You also might describe the identity of the Dutch architect today through the presence of Rem Koolhaas.

FM You mean without him there wouldn't be such a thing?

JM Yes, because he is such an important architect and theoretician. Although his writings do not have the form of theory, there is a lot of theory in them, especially in *Delirious New York*.

The book, subtitled a 'retro active manifesto for New York', is an exploration of the relationship between the forces of the metropolis (in this case New York City) and architecture. Written in 1978, it set the stage for OMA's ground-breaking work of the 1980s. Koolhaas is the first rock 'n' roll architect. He made the profession 'chic' and has brought it to an inter-disciplinary status that encompasses art, urbanism, fashion and the media. However, the brilliance of OMA was not achieved single-handedly. The exhibition 'Reference "OMA"', held in 1995 at The Netherlands Architecture Institute (NAI) in Rotterdam, examined former students and collaborators of OMA who influenced the office, most of whom are currently finding fame on their own. Kees Christiaanse, Willem Jan Neutelings, Christian Rapp, Winy Maas and Rients Dijkstra were among the first generation that graduated from the 'university of OMA'.

Only a few years after most of these practices were formed, a second wave of architectural collectives such as NOX, S.333, NL Architects and Bosch Haslett were established. They did not work for OMA, but were influenced directly by the *modus operandi* of the, by now, legendary office. Riding the wave of the building boom in The Netherlands, these new offices went on to produce some of the most exciting projects. Their work can be described as an enlightened pragmatism that acknowledges the economic, political or social constraints architecture has to face today. 'Nine Plus One', a series of exhibitions held at the NAi in 1997, highlights the achievements of this generation. What they all have in common is a cunning ability to combine the quality (or sometimes absurdness or strangeness) of their proposals with seductive visuals during their presentations. These media strategies paved the way for an unprecedented amount of interest by the press:

KB Every time I open an architectural publication it's the same group of architects who are written about. As a writer I feel badly for the ones who are excluded. I realise it's an issue of quality, but I think there's also a hype around certain architects.

Maarten Kloos It's absolutely a hype. Sometimes you feel that the hype is correct. I mean the excitement around the work of MVRDV, that's a correct hype at the moment. Especially the WOZOCOS in Amsterdam, the house in Utrecht, and the VPRO in Hilversum. That's correct, it's absolutely something new and very amusing, and it's very youthful, full of energy. And in another five years maybe there are other ones.

It remains to be seen if the works that are admired and loved today will be regarded as architectural dinosaurs in years to come, perhaps as little as 10 years. Judging from the quantity of noteworthy projects produced over the past 7 years, any reassessment would take the scope of historical research.

ACKNOWLEDGEMENTS
We thank the Stimuleringsfond voor Architectuur in Rotterdam for their generous support; the Nederlandse Spoorwegen who gave us railway passes to travel across The Netherlands to conduct our research; the Dutch embassy in London; The Netherlands' Architecture Institute for access to their library; and all the architects who took time to answer our questions and for the wealth of material provided: there are too many to list here.

A few but essential conversations raised our awareness of the cultural scope of Dutch architecture: without Bart Lootsma we would have remained ignorant of the political and economic mechanisms of the country; Maarten Kloos gave sound advice on processing the overwhelming amount of information; and Joost Meuwissen and Mathijs Bouw of One Architecture granted the most entertaining discussion on architecture, which made some sections in this book possible.

Special thanks to Tom Neville for his patience and support, and to Gerrie van Noord for her assistance in editing the book.

Florian Migsch thanks his parents for their help and commitment over the book's gestation. Kathy Battista thanks her family and friends for their support throughout the duration of the project.
FM and KB February 1998

Using this book

This guide divides the 12 provinces of The Netherlands into ten parts, including separate sections on Amsterdam and Rotterdam. While most of the buildings are accessible by public transport, some are easily reached on bicycle. Bicycles can be rented for a small fee at every train station and at various places in major cities. The few locations that demand extensive bus or tram journeys also have the nearest motorway listed to provide a number of possible routes.

We recommend the widely available Falk maps, as they are far superior to any others: the Tourist Board, or VVV, also publishes practical maps, and local branches should be your first point of reference. Almost every person we met spoke excellent English, which is good news for all visitors without a command of Dutch. Members of staff of the VVV are no exception and, unsurprisingly, they are knowledgeable about recent buildings in their neighbourhood.

Many buildings documented here are abbreviated or nicknamed by the locals: as far as is possible, these names have been included.

Amsterdam

New Metropolis	16
Ibis Hotel and Wagon Lits	20
Sjoerd Soeters architectural office	22
Byzantium	24
Van Gogh Museum extension	26
GWL terrain	28
WOZOCO	34
Eurotwin Business Centre	38
Bezaanjachtplein housing	42
Twiske West residential neighbourhood	44
Borneo Sporenburg urban development	46
Piraeus apartment block	50
Piet Hein Tunnel	54
Amsterdam Arena	56
International School of Amsterdam	60
CoBrA Museum, Amstelveen	62
Schiphol Airport Terminal West, World Trade Centre and Plaza	64

New Metropolis

Although the New Metropolis looks like a giant green ship moored to an eastern dock in Amsterdam's harbour, the Italian maestro of architecture and design, Renzo Piano, did not intend it to be so. The building is in fact a science museum. Harry Meijer, project manager in The Netherlands, discussed this aspect of the design:

Harry Meijer He doesn't care about this. The ship metaphor was not there. It was more like a small slope down into a dark hole where you're always afraid that someone has broken down or a car accident or water is coming to you. Being afraid of a dark area and he wants to make the opposite – light. That was his first sketch. A very small sketch.

FM Was he very closely involved with the detailing?

HM The thing with Renzo Piano is he always makes his own building in each place. He's never making the same detail.

Piano's idea was to make a building that responded to its location directly above the IJ tunnel (which was built in 1968). According to Olaf de Nooyer, project architect, the form was indeed a reaction to the surroundings. As the tunnel curves, so must the building. Because cars are literally 'swallowed' into the water Piano wanted to counteract this movement by making the building rise up on the IJ side. The resulting steep plane of the roof, which faces south, logically cried out for a dual function. The sun deck, accessed via a gangway, functions as a public square and exhibition space raised to roof level. The most fantastic moment in the building is looking back at the old city of Amsterdam. A view north, to the newer developments, is not permitted because of the high safety railings and closed access to the tip of the building, or what could be described as the bow of a boat.

Renzo Piano Workshop 1990–97

Amsterdam

Renzo Piano Workshop 1990–97

The name 'New Metropolis' was chosen by the director of the museum, who was inspired by Fritz Lang's classic film *Metropolis* of 1927, the ultimate architecture film. The decision not to call it a science museum could be risky considering the need for half a million paying visitors each year to keep it financially viable. Despite any confusion about its nautical theme, the museum is in fact a science centre that focuses on education with interactive exhibits on technology and industry. Once inside, however, the interior is uninspired. There is no light because all exhibits are spotlit and daylight would only distract a visitor. The real focus is the exterior, the excitement stemming from the accessible roof and the view of the building from afar. It seems that the director of the museum, who flew to Italy to woo Piano into taking the commission, was concerned more with the architecture than with the exhibits. In any case, the building is certainly a great asset to Amsterdam and is a positive sign that things outside the mainstream are being built close to the centre.

ADDRESS Oosterdock, Amsterdam
GETTING THERE BUS 22 to Kadijksplein, or turn left out of Centraal Station and walk for 5 minutes
ACCESS open; entrance fee

Renzo Piano Workshop 1990–97

Amsterdam

Renzo Piano Workshop 1990–97

Ibis Hotel and Wagon Lits

The most romantic way of entering Amsterdam is by train, arriving at Centraal Station, a grand example of historical Dutch architecture. Situated to the west of the railway embankment is a recent project by Jan Benthem and Mels Crouwel, the architects who have brilliantly refurbished Schiphol Airport (see page 64). The complex consists of a tall office building juxtaposed with a rectangular block of hotel rooms and a pedestrian and cyclists bridge. On the ground floor a strip with public amenities, such as a restaurant and shops, links the two volumes.

The most striking feature is the differentiation in façades of the two buildings. The vertical element contains a semicircular office tower on stilts with alternating levels of service balconies and slatted aluminium sun shades. Connected to this is the external elevator and stairwell shaft that allow maximum floor space in the tower. Serving as a counterpart to its neighbour, the hotel's façade consists of an undulating face of reflective glass brick. Here bathrooms are set against the outer wall in the French *wagons-lit* style.

Amsterdam

ADDRESS Stationsplein, Amsterdam
GETTING THERE turn right immediately on leaving Centraal Station
ACCESS hotel open

Benthem Crouwel Architecten bv 1992

Benthem Crouwel Architecten bv 1992

Sjoerd Soeters architectural office

It is perhaps fitting that the office of the architect who has been called 'the naughtiest boy in the class' is located on a street where a magic mushroom establishment neighbours cartoon and clubgear shops. Sjoerd Soeters has converted a former church to an office that embodies his funloving and irreverent approach to architecture. The corrugated steel façade topped by a bulging cornice marks the original location, which has at its core a large void lit by a skylight. It is here that one is received into the building and here that the office takes its daily communal lunch.

Soeters' headquarters has spilled over into two other Dutch-style apartment buildings. The two, large, circular objects on the adjoining cornice are actually tyres painted white, reflecting the rhythm of the buildings on the street. Soeters' sarcasm is aimed at the increasingly problematic parking situation in the city centre. Unfortunately, the joke was not well received at the outset. Soeters elaborates:

Sjoerd Soeters In The Netherlands if you make jokes, you are not part of the upper culture. If you make a joke, then you step out, you are not reliable. And that's one of the reasons why I want to make jokes, because I think people love this. The whole street hated me for this, I was a pariah in the street for five years, and people who I had never met before suddenly came and shook my hand and said, 'You have made a very nice building'. It is a definite separation among people, so I tried to serve them both, because they both have a good reason for the system.

ADDRESS Kerkstraat 204, Amsterdam
TRAM 16, 24, 25 from Centraal Station
ACCESS none

Amsterdam

Architectenbureau Soeters 1988–89

Architectenbureau Soeters 1988–89

Byzantium

When we – still members of the uninitiated public – strolled past Byzantium near the hectic Leidseplein, we joked that this must be the work of an admirer of OMA. It had some of the handwriting of the architectural powerhouse from Rotterdam, but we thought it lacked the brilliance that ennobles their œuvre. To our embarrassment it was not the spark of Rem Koolhaas' intellect that was amiss but our pre-rites-of-passage status, before being transformed into fans of The Netherlands' most unloved architectural talent.

Rem Koolhaas, whose biting sarcasm and polemics on architecture have elevated him to the status of an intercontinental celebrity, presented the project a decade after he received the commission in a comic strip drawn by his son. The cartoon, part of *S,M,L,XL*, Rem's 3-kilogram bible on himself, elucidates the battles a metropolitan architect has to endure with the evil forces of single-minded developers before successfully delivering the manna to the people. Byzantium is all about glamorous shopping in the golden wedge which serves as its plinth, doing business in the offices above, and enjoying the location of the apartments overlooking Europe's dog- and rollerblade-infested Vondell Park. The pop quality of Tomas Koolhaas' narrative betrays the actual sobriety of the building. It epitomises what his father once said in an interview: 'For me the most attractive proposition was to build essentially very unpretentious intelligent ... relatively elegant, but also relatively neutral things.'

ADDRESS Stadhouderskade, Zandpad, Amsterdam
CLIENT Parkstede (MBO, Bouwfonds, Ballast Nedam)
DESIGN TEAM Rem Koolhaas, Kees Christiaanse, Ron Steiner
TRAM 1, 2, 5, 6, 7, 10, 11 BUS 170, 171, 172 to Leidseplein
ACCESS public amenities only

Office for Metropolitan Architecture 1985–91

Amsterdam

Office for Metropolitan Architecture 1985–91

Van Gogh Museum extension

Redevelopment of the Museumplein has caused much controversy. Each plan is met with scrutiny from a host of bodies including the city and local councils, local residents, cultural institutions, and shop keepers. Add this volatile situation to the precarious task of adding to a building by Rietveld, a master of modernism, and the result is a very tricky commission for any architect. Kisho Kurokawa (the Rem Koolhaas of the east) has used grace under pressure to come up with a plan that integrates function and beauty, without antagonising the original structure.

The choice of architect is, in essence, the result of Japan's love affair with Vincent van Gogh. The museum is the most famous European museum in Japan – about 30 per cent of its audience are Japanese. *Sunflowers*, probably Van Gogh's most famous painting, was bought by a Japanese man for NFL60 million and, perhaps feeling a tad guilty about removing a treasure from its home country, he gave NFL35 million toward the extension. So it is no surprise that a Japanese architect was chosen.

After 6 years construction has finally started. Kurokawa's plan involved a new building behind the original museum, the two connected by an underground passage. Though originally conceived as a round structure, the extension has been changed to an oval (and placed closer to the original building) after complaints from Sven-Ingvar Andersson, the Danish landscape architect responsible for the new Museumplein. Because Kurokawa's oval is an independent structure, the museum will only have to close for 6 months, when the most famous paintings will be on exhibition in the new wing of the Rijksmuseum by Wim Quist.

ADDRESS Paulus Potterstraat 7, Amsterdam
TRAM 2, 5 BUS 145, 170, 197 to Museumplein
ACCESS open; entrance fee

Kisho Kurokawa Architects & Associates 1996–98

Amsterdam

Kisho Kurokawa Architects & Associates 1996–98

GWL terrain

Amsterdam not only has a strong tradition in public-sector housing, but also in grass-roots politics, manifested most vocally in the squatter movement of the 1980s. Now the former squatters have become academics or are involved in local politics. Not surprisingly their sense of community is deeply engrained in the powerful local district authority (*stadsdeelbestuur*), and councils frequently adopt a planning policy that looks beyond the cost calculation of developers and encourages unorthodox (i.e. non-profitable) urban proposals.

After the decommissioning of the Municipal Water Board (GWL), Westerpark's authority earmarked the site for the development of an environmentally friendly neighbourhood. Kees Christiaanse Architects won an invited competition in 1992 and were subsequently chosen as urban planners. Their design had to accommodate the enormous density of 100 apartments per hectare, half of them financed by the free market. Without public subsidies, developers tend to avoid risks, relying on opportunistic dwelling types that are cheap to build and easy to sell. Christiaanse's office opted for a mixture of straightforward apartment buildings, which sneak along the perimeter of the site, and a group of 15 loosely positioned, free-standing blocks inside. The blocks' orientation continues the street grid of the neighbouring Staatslieden quarter, the only difference being that vehicles are excluded, with paths between for pedestrians use.

The virtually car-free development was one part of the environmental policy of the urban plan. It allowed a maximum of 0.3 vehicles per apartment, with the parking lots for the 200-odd cars hidden behind two large apartment 'walls'. Another important feature was the allocation of a private garden to dwellings without direct access to the ground. While this turned out to be infeasible – there was simply not enough space – most inhabitants were assigned a piece of greenery. Landscape architects

Amsterdam

Kees Christiaanse Architects and Planners (masterplan) 1992–94

Amsterdam

Kees Christiaanse Architects and Planners (masterplan) 1992–94

West 8 surrounded these allotments with deep, low hedges. A curious rule aims to homogenise the open space: any man-made constructions more than 1.2 metres high are forbidden. Owners are encouraged to grow trees and vegetables, but are not allowed to have anything higher than a bench.

The urban plan set several criteria for the architecture. Circulation had to be retained in the blocks, no external entrance galleries being allowed. As many apartments as possible were to have access to the ground or, failing that, to a roof garden. DKV were commissioned to design the large apartment block shielding the site's western edge; the winding volume and its gently rising roof line were prescribed by Christiaanse. The integrated roof gardens resulted in a series of terraces that step down to the south. As the building rises, the access corridors that continue horizontally from their respective terraces make a variety of dwelling types possible, while also excavating a series of communal courtyards from the building mass.

But the real typological renewal came from two architectural offices: Atelier Zeinstra/van der Pol and Neutelings Riedijk Architecten. Both offices exploited the rule to include either a garden or a roof terrace to such an extent that some apartments stretched over five storeys. The biggest constraint the architects had to overcome was the so-called tunnel construction technique: with this method apartment blocks are built as a vertical grid of rectangular concrete boxes. Although bound to this technique, both offices successfully circumvented the extruded spatial impression of a 'tunnel'. Liesbeth van der Pol told us of the fights she and her colleagues had with the developers over the issue of unconventional entrance and access patterns. Her proposal took two interlocked apartments as the base unit for the block. As each dwelling moves up a storey their orientation switches from one-half of the plan to the other. Therefore an apartment that started with a south garden would culminate on the

Kees Christiaanse Architects and Planners (masterplan) 1992–94

Kees Christiaanse Architects and Planners (masterplan) 1992–94

fifth floor with a north-facing roof terrace, and vice versa.

Michiel Riedijk, on the other hand, invented a three-dimensional space puzzle involving four intertwined apartments per block section. The modest exterior betrays the complex internal organisation, yet the basic principle is simple. Riedijk divided the plans into three zones: a strip for kitchen/dining, a central band of staircases (one for each flat) and a zone for bedrooms. He then calculated the necessary number of bedrooms and living rooms for each unit and connected them with the kitchen and staircase via a succession of levels. Each apartment has its own entrance on the ground floor, but an entirely different interior. While some types have the rooms concentrated on the last two floors, others (like Van der Pol's) are distributed evenly throughout the full height. The configuration of the apartments can be adapted to changing lifestyle patterns.

The GWL terrain is remarkable for a number of reasons, most notably for the political support that made a number of curious dwelling types possible. The project development involved urban planners, landscape architects and an environmental engineering consultancy, which the Dutch shrug off as business as usual. Their capacity for integrating specialists as part of the multi-disciplinary design team can only be envied from an Anglo-Saxon perspective where King Mammon rules urban development, and consequently architecture.

ADDRESS Van Hogendorpstraat, Van Hallstraat, Amsterdam-Westerpark
ARCHITECTS Atelier Zeinstra/van der Pol, Kees Christiaanse Architects and Planners, DKV Architecten, Meyer & Van Schoten, Neutelings Riedijk Architecten bv
CONSULTANTS BOOM Environmental Consultants
TRAM 10 BUS 18 to van Hallstraat ACCESS footpaths only

Amsterdam

Kees Christiaanse Architects and Planners (masterplan) 1992–94

Amsterdam

Kees Christiaanse Architects and Planners (masterplan) 1992–94

WOZOCO

This housing project is simply the most exciting and hysterical thing in Dutch architecture at the moment. Everyone in Holland is talking about it. It has graced the front pages of everything from architecture journals to the *Volkskrant*, one of the leading newspapers of Holland. It embodies the energy, enthusiasm, and ingenuity of the new generation of architects in The Netherlands.

The building is located in Osdorp, a nondescript residential area in west Amsterdam where blocks from the 1950s and 1960s stand as testaments to the monotony of modernity. MVRDV was given the commission to design 100 dwellings for the elderly in the social sector (Woonzorg complex). The architects decided to have the footprint of a building, a slab, as thin as possible so that the communal area would be as large as possible. The strict budget limited the size of each house and, because of height regulations, it was discovered that only 87 dwellings could fit in each slab.

Winy Maas There were thirteen houses left. What shall we do with them? A building on the ground floor would spoil the sensation of communal space. So we said, let's keep them in the air. Let's suspend it. And then the space continues and exists.

KB Were there a lot of restrictions when you wanted to build out, in the air?

WM Well, yes, we had some problems, like who is occupying the air? When you have it cantilevered the ground underneath should be occupied by the owner as well. Or not. So that took a while to organise.

KB You had to fight for it?

WM … the client was fantastic. He helped a lot. Politically it was fantastic as well. When the Alderman saw it he wanted it. The ones in between

MVRDV 1994–97

MVRDV 1994–97

were the heavy ones, like the fire guys. But in the end it worked out.

As the cantilevered apartments could not be aligned at the same level because of planning regulations about the amount of light, the protrusions in fact are staggered throughout the façade and are suspended by flexible steel beams which give slightly when the inhabitants pace about.

WM It goes up and down of course. That is part of the sensation of it.
FM You mean you really feel it?
WM Yes, you feel it but that's okay. When you don't feel it, you don't have the idea that you are living in a house like that. You should feel it, but to a certain extent. You shouldn't get seasick in it. And not be frightened. But a slight shiver is fantastic.
FM A slight trickle of eroticism.
WM Exactly.

In social housing in The Netherlands it is traditional that future occupants are allowed to choose one aspect of their dwelling. Owing to a lack of funds, the architects could only allow the tenants to choose the colour of their balcony. The resulting kaleidoscope effect of purple, orange, green, yellow and steel-mesh balconies adds to the hysteria of the project and makes it a fun building.

ADDRESS Reimerswaalstraat/Ookmeerweg, Amsterdam
PROJECT ARCHITECTS Winy Maas, Jacob van Rijs, Nathalie de Vries
CLIENT Woningbouwvereniging Het Oosten
BUS 23 to Osdorper Ban
ACCESS none

Amsterdam

MVRDV 1994–97

MVRDV 1994–97

Eurotwin Business Centre

Usually areas of light industry on the outskirts of cities are quite predictable: non-descript, lifeless buildings which add to the monotony of the surroundings. In the north of Amsterdam Claus en Kaan Architekten have executed an exceptional project that breaks out of the dullness of its quasi-industrial brief. Combining offices and workshop premises, with programmes spanning from Ray's American Donuts to contemporary furniture designers, the Eurotwin combines elegance and functionalism in understated forms.

The complex has a tower and a low-rise element that is mirrored on the site. The high-rise buildings, which contain offices, are clad in vertical slabs of neutral-coloured timber. Connected to these are workshops housed in a series of low-rise sheds, also timber-clad but this time with horizontal planks. The sumptuous material – Red Cedar covered in linseed oil – is surprisingly subtle, even giving the buildings an appearance of concrete from a distance. The simplicity of the forms and the horizontal windows suggest that Felix Claus and Cees Kaan were looking to their modernist predecessors for inspiration. However, they do not acknowledge any such connection but attribute their work instead to a strict refining of style:

Felix Claus You know the Dutch discourse about modernism and what modernism is. At the moment there are critics who say a lot of architects are still working in this modernist tradition. We have always felt that this is a mute issue. There is no such thing as modernist style. Modernism is a vernacular. When we started out we wanted to put as much energy as possible into the buildings themselves. After having studied and worked on housing projects for ten years having the chance to build something you really focus and want to do it as perfect as

Claus en Kaan Architecten 1992–93

Claus en Kaan Architecten 1992–93

possible. Of course this doesn't explain the geometry and the simplicity. That has more to do with our urge to find what's essential in it. We are not happy until we find the solution that is the only one that can be drawn. It sounds quite obvious but it's really not that obvious. Many times we are working on projects and we find that you can have several solutions for the problem. We review the concept, rework it, find the essence, and then go back. It's to do with trying to get the buildings free from all the associations we know. Trying to get the buildings to stand for themselves.

Amsterdam

ADDRESS Paperverweg, Amsterdam Noord
PROJECT ARCHITECTS Felix Claus, Cees Kaan
BUS 39e from Centraal Station
ACCESS none

Claus en Kaan Architecten 1992–93

Claus en Kaan Architecten 1992–93

Bezaanjachtplein housing

'The cities of the nineties demand an approach that is urbane as opposed to urban' argue John Bosch and Gordon Haslett of the young office Bosch Haslett. Their *savoir-faire* attitude plucks the benefits of a cosmopolitan culture, while it abstains from the negative by-effects. The firm's sophistication becomes evident in breathtakingly beautiful models and project folders, whose chic simplicity won them the competition 'Anders Bouwen, Anders Wonen' (Design Differently, Dwell Differently).

The resulting commission, which was their first realised design, is a modest block of 28 maisonettes located in the north of Amsterdam. Faced with a generic context of apartment slabs that are beyond reform, the formal expression restrains itself to the plain but elegant colours and materials. Their interpretation of the building regulations, which fixed the ratio of window surface to floor area, led to a deep apartment type with fully glazed façades at both ends. The maisonettes, which were left unfinished inside, allow occupants the chance to define their own living environments. The housing, referred to by Bosch Haslett as 'social lofts', lives up to the architects' reputation for producing a combination of flexible and elegant design while staying within the constraints of social housing.

ADDRESS Bezaanjachtplein, Amsterdam Noord
DESIGN TEAM John Bosch, Gordon Haslett, Gerard Kruunenberg, Paul van der Erve
SIZE 28 maisonettes for the social sector
BUS 34 to Bezaanjachtplein
ACCESS none

Amsterdam

Bosch Haslett 1991–93

Bosch Haslett 1991–93

Twiske West residential neighbourhood

A housing project by Liesbeth van der Pol in the north of Amsterdam is emblematic of the self-assurance and innovative approach to housing embraced by the younger generation of Dutch architects. Comprising 212 social-sector rented houses, the development is split in two sections: areas with five single-family houses grouped around internal courtyards, which stresses the social aspect of such a neighbourhood; and three sets of four circular buildings set on a canal, each with seven dwellings set around an open core to interconnect residents in a more subtle arrangement. Liesbeth van der Pol spoke about the play between these types of housing:

> For me it's the difference between the two characters. The one enclosing squares, while the circles are the objects standing free in the space. There's such a difference between the two. I want to build these differences so that you can pick out what is for you. On the one hand we had to make squares and we also had to make objects. Nothing is more object-like to me than a circle. It was quite evident to me to make it a circle, also in contrast to the built squares.

In the circular buildings the architect cleverly rotated each level of the stacked dwellings to give variations in natural light. Thus, a bedroom on the top floor will have a different view from that of the kitchen at ground-floor level. The neighbourhood represents an innovative and humanistic approach to subsidised housing.

ADDRESS Nesserhoek, Coehornerhoek, Schelvischhoofd, Amsterdam
BUS 92 from Centraal Station
ACCESS public areas only

Amsterdam

Atelier Zeinstra/van der Pol 1991–93

Atelier Zeinstra/van der Pol 1991–93

Borneo Sporenburg urban development

West 8's presentation drawings resemble pop art assemblages where images from everyday life are juxtaposed artificially in a manner presumed to be eye-catching. One collage for the Borneo Sporenburg project in east Amsterdam shows a patio directly over the Piet Hein tunnel with a view of the harbour. The idyllic scene with, for example, a couple draped luxuriously over deckchairs, an out-of-proportion bulldog and a gargantuan flowerpot, is foiled by urban traits such as the aluminium mesh of the patio and the grim skyline, but it is essentially a play between pastoral bliss and urban context.

The developers of the Borneo Sporenburg wanted to cater for the demands of the real estate market by offering an alternative to the suburbs at this attractive waterside site. The two narrow islands are removed from the centre of the city, which appeals to wannabe suburbanites, but the proximity of the inner city is appealing and convenient. New Deal, a conglomerate agency of four housing corporations and three contractors, chose West 8 as the masterplanners and the landscape architects faced a challenging brief: 2500 dwellings on two former piers; and of these 70 per cent had to have direct street access while 50 per cent had to have private parking facilities. The resulting density was 100 dwellings per hectare. Adriaan Geuze and Wim Kloosterboer of West 8 decided to undermine the position of masterplanner by allowing the commissioned architects to solve problems in stimulating and ingenious ways and in an interesting twist they assigned the difficult areas to younger and innovative offices. Also the more conventional firms were encouraged to compete so that the architecture produced would be more stimulating.

West 8's general solution was to make a variety of housing styles to exploit the concept of a life by the water's edge. Their design consisted of interminable rows of three-storey volumes offset by nodal points of

Amsterdam

West 8 Landscape Architects 1993–98

Amsterdam

West 8 Landscape Architects 1993–98

higher blocks which work as sculptural references and offer occupants fantastic views of the area. Public infrastructure is also kept to a minimum – there are no shops on the islands – so allowing maximum land coverage for residential use. Superfluous space is eliminated by keeping street widths to a minimum between developments and by giving residents intimate and private patios and roof gardens.

ADDRESS Borneo and Sporenburg Islands, Amsterdam
PROJECT ARCHITECTS Adriaan Geuze, Wim Kloosterboer, Yushi Uehara, Sebastiaan Riquois
PARTICIPATING ARCHITECTS S Beel, Van Berkel & Bos, CASA, Kees Christiaanse, Claus en Kaan, DKV, EEA, FARO, X de Geyteer, Van Goor, Heren 5, Van Herk & De Klein, Herzog & de Meuron, Höhne & Rapp, Steven Holl, Inbo, JA Atelier, Kother & Salman, LRRH, Marge, Mastenbroek van Gameren/De Architectengroep, J L Mateo, Neutelings Riedijk, OMA, R Petersma, Atelier Zeinstra/van der Pol, M Rohmer, Van Sambeek & Van Veen, S Sorgdrager, Stuurman & Partners, Tangram, Tupker & Van de Neut, Koen van Velsen, R Visser,
CLIENT New Deal Stichting BO 1, SFB, Smits Bouwbedrijf, Bouwbedrijf M J de Nijs
BUS 28, 32, 59, 61 to Ertskade
ACCESS open

West 8 Landscape Architects 1993–98

West 8 Landscape Architects 1993–98

Piraeus apartment block

Since the 1960s late-capitalism has changed western European cities, driving out manufacturing and heavy industry from their centres. A parallel process of urbanisation has taken over these brownfield sites and transformed them into residential districts for a new urban middle class. Unable to deliver further growth in the centre of Amsterdam, housing associations encroached on the vast deserted harbours of the eastern periphery. Their policy created new dwellings for an insatiable market, and the redevelopments represent an exercise in the latest in urban planning. In his masterplan for the KNSM island in the Oostelijk Havengebied, Jo Coenen envisaged a string of monumental apartment blocks that mimic the former warehouses while retaining the few remnants of that time.

The most remarkable design of the quintet of architectural firms invited is that of Hans Kollhoff and Christian Rapp's apartment block, Piraeus. Rapp, who worked for Kollhoff at that time, now runs his own architectural offices in Amsterdam and Berlin. His most recent projects in The Netherlands led to the unprecedented giving of the renowned Maskaant Price award to a foreign practitioner. Yet the Piraeus block is clearly in the style of Kollhoff who was inspired by H P Berlage and followers of the Amsterdam School.

The vast volume contains 300 apartments and integrates a listed harbour building in a tender, though intimidating embrace. What is impressive about this fantastic sculptural spectacle is the malleability of the building's mass and angular frame. As a side effect of the tweaked tectonic, the inhabitants could choose their flats from a legion of different floorplans and apartment typologies. Spatially, the most unusual of these are under the slanted roof where large glass panels give them the semblance of warehouse lofts. The sheer size of the block and the presence

Amsterdam

Hans Kollhoff, Christian Rapp/masterplan Jo Coenen 1989–94

Amsterdam

Hans Kollhoff, Christian Rapp/masterplan Jo Coenen 1989–94

of a variety of workspaces, shops and a café along Levantkade give an urban feel to the development, a theme also echoed in the sophisticated detailing of the various entrances and windows. In one passage through the inner yard, artist Arno van der Mark duplicated the existing supporting columns of Kollhoff's design and gave them plaques whose imprinted cuttings from city maps thematise the passage as an urban metaphor.

Piraeus' bulking mass is clad in a deep red brick whose texture and hermetic appearance represents a truly Germanic reading of Berlage. Nothing disturbs the introvertedness of the volume and its finely proportioned window grid. Most of the balconies do not protrude from the façade, effectively being walled-in winter gardens. Replacing the expressive small-scale brickwork details of Berlage's contemporaries with the sweeping gesture of angled elevations, Kollhoff's architecture is too reminiscent of the paintings of the Italian surrealist Giorgio de Chirico's paintings to be enjoyable. At night time, the endless perimeter of the building and its daunting prospect evoke a feeling of de Chirico's sensibility, one that was ridden with city-angst, bare of any hope for salvation.

ADDRESS KNSM Laan, Amsterdam
PROJECT ARCHITECT Christian Rapp
INVITED FIRMS Casa, B Albert, F and P Wintermans, W Arets, J Crepain
CLIENT Woonstichting De Doelen, Amsterdam
SIZE 304 apartments, 95 per cent for social rental sector
BUS 28, 32, 59, 61 to KNSM Laan
ACCESS to public amenities only

Hans Kollhoff, Christian Rapp/masterplan Jo Coenen 1989–94

Amsterdam

Amsterdam

Hans Kollhoff, Christian Rapp/masterplan Jo Coenen 1989–94

Piet Hein Tunnel

Ben van Berkel and Caroline Bos explain their work as an intense reading of existing urban forces found in vehicle flows, topography or view lines. The inherent dynamic of this method makes it suitable for utilitarian buildings such as the Piet Hein tunnel in east Amsterdam. This piece of infrastructure provides a strategically important link between the new residential district in Borneo Sporenburg (page 46) and the A10 ring road. A drive through the tunnel at night is an exhilarating experience of the architecture of speed. The purity of the architects' idea is best conveyed by the two ventilation buildings that guard the entrances. Their gleaming concrete and steel decor made me think of the Italian futurists who, intoxicated by progress, announced the age of all-smashing velocity.

FM Your office is pretty special for tackling both utility or engineering commissions as well as pure architectural designs. Do you think that both roles can inform each other and bring on new solutions? A kind of synergy?

Ben van Berkel Some of my tutors at the Architectural Association [in London] were studying large-scale engineering projects in that period, and I come a little bit from that background, so these aspects of architecture engineering and design have always been my interest ... The new techniques of working we believe are important, to combine these different disciplines, but also we like to use each other's effects sometimes.

ADDRESS Piet Hein tunnel, ventilation houses at Cornelius van Eesterenlaan (west) and Zuider IJdijk (east)
BUS 59, 61 to Ertskade for west end; 37 to Zuiderzeeweg for east end
ACCESS open

Amsterdam

Van Berkel & Bos Architecten bv 1990–97

Amsterdam

Van Berkel & Bos Architecten bv 1990–97

Amsterdam Arena

The French anthropologist Marc Augé states that Western society spends an increasing part of its life in highly organised transient settings, such as the mall, airport or leisure centre. These are urban nodes in a way of life that Auge refers to as supermodern. One cultural artefact of this super-modernity is the sports arena, which brackets our civic desires, from athletic events to rock concerts. The Amsterdam Arena is not a conventional football ground but a mega interior with skyboxes, VIP areas and media facilities that beam pay-per-view football to viewers around the globe.

Getting to the stadium by car is easy as it is built above a four-lane motorway: two parking decks have 2600 parking places. Conceived as a general-purpose arena, the pit is surrounded by a concrete moat which allows buses and heavy vehicles to enter. To be independent of the unpredictabilities of the weather, engineering consultants Grabowski & Poort designed a vaulted roof that spans an impressive 177 metres. Its football field-sized middle section can be slid open, yet the arched structure is not fully resolved as the points between the secondary roof trusses and the square perimeter of the opening look rather inelegant. The function of the oversized bowls on the four supporting columns remains a mystery. Are they rainwater collectors or satellite dishes?

Squeezed between the double balconies of stands and the external circulation ring, the commercial premises capitalise on the passing crowds. This main concourse is accessed via two sets of staircases situated at the ends of the oval placed behind perforated concrete screens by Sjoerd Soeters, the Arena's joint architect.

The Ajax museum, also Soeters' work, is set in front of the stadium. Hot dogs and beer meet the slick corrugated steel of inner-city bars. Although the museum building straddles the motorway, the triumphal

ir. Rob Schuurman, Grabowski & Poort 1990–96

Amsterdam

ir. Rob Schuurman, Grabowski & Poort 1990–96

arch reference assumes an air of nostalgia, looking displaced as a gateway in front of the 60-metre-high stadium rotunda.

All functions apart from the basic pitch–stand relationship are externalised and added into, under and on top of the concrete structure. The opportunity to fuse the complex programmes into a compressed urbanism in the spirit of OMA has been omitted in favour of aestheticising the various architectural elements.

In the age of satellite-TV football, where the meaning of the stadium as a social place is discredited, a structure like the Arena can be found in any European metropolitan area. It is the inability to draw on the location and its failure to arouse any emotions that render the Amsterdam Arena devoid of a character.

ADDRESS Burgemeester Stramanweg, Amsterdam
JOINT ARCHITECT Sjoerd Soeters
CLIENT Stadion Amsterdam nv, Dienst Parkeerbeheer
METRO 54 to Strandvliet
BUS 29, 59, 60, 60S, 137, 158, 174, 175 to Bijlmer
CAR A2, Ouderkerk a/d Amstel exit
ACCESS only during events

ir. Rob Schuurman, Grabowski & Poort 1990–96

ir. Rob Schuurman, Grabowski & Poort 1990–96

International School of Amsterdam

Margaret Armstrong-Law, director of the International School of Amsterdam, which caters for international students aged between 3 and 19 years, invited a small group of architects to submit proposals for the design of a new campus. Ton Alberts and Max van Huut were the clear winners and subsequently were given the responsibility for creating a new home for the school. Their idea was to build an environment based on a clustered classroom system, which is organised according to age for lower and middle schools, and by discipline for the upper school. By placing common rooms in the centre of each cluster the architects stressed the importance of socialising as well as the flexibility of their plan, emphasising what they call 'organic architecture', but which seems more influenced by the anthroposophic teachings of Rudolf Steiner.

The single-storey school rises to three floors in the library area and recalls a castle from a fairy tale. The two-tone, red brick cladding is a trademark of the architects (it is also found in their GasUnie building in Groningen (page 116) and the one-family house in Amersfoort) as is the unusual shape of the building, a result of their belief that square and rectangular rooms prohibit creativity. The building seems to reiterate for the school's motto: 'strive for excellence by learning problem-solving skills'.

Amsterdam

ADDRESS Spoortslaan
PROJECT ARCHITECT Ton Alberts, Max van Huut
COST NFL40 million, with landscaping
METRO 5, 51 to Spoortslaan
ACCESS only by appointment

Architectenbureau Alberts & van Huut 1993–96

Architectenbureau Alberts & van Huut 1993–96

CoBrA Museum, Amstelveen

In Amstelveen, a southern suburb of Amsterdam, the centre square (named after CoBrA promoter Willem Sandberg) is being torn up for new buildings which it is hoped will rejuvenate the area. The CoBrA Museum, designed by Wim Quist, is the first building completed in the urban ensemble. Quist, who seems to have a monopoly over Dutch museum commissions, employs his clean, sober style to create a suitable home for the collection of over 300 works of the twentieth-century CoBrA (Copenhagen, Brussels, Amsterdam) art movement.

The building confronts the city from a number of directions: the brick and glass angular façade faces the urban sector on two fronts, while to the rear of the museum glass walls front a canal and address the more serene side of the plot which has water and greenery. Once inside the building the public areas, bookshop and café greet the visitor immediately. These areas are juxtaposed with the glass of the façade, thus creating a discourse with the new square development.

Quist rotated the axis of the first floor 45° in relation to the ground floor, resulting in an unobstructed flow of light from all directions. Additional light is also provided by a circular glass patio to the centre of the building where a Japanese artist has created a Zen garden. Much like Quist's Museum in Scheveningen, the strength of the CoBrA building is the sobriety and solidity of the design.

ADDRESS Sandbergplein 1-3, Amstelveen
PROJECT ARCHITECT W G Quist
LANDSCAPE ARCHITECT Gemeente Amstelveen
BUS 125, 147, 170, 172, 173, 174, 193 to Sandbergplein, Amstelveen
ACCESS open

Architektenburo Quist bv 1992–96

Amsterdam

Architektenburo Quist bv 1992–96

Schiphol Airport Terminal West, World Trade Centre and Plaza

Airports are the new cities of our time with a population subjected to a jet-lagged and transitory existence based on notions of temporality and instability. In spite of this relativity, their geopolitical position is a decisive factor in the international ambitions of the economies to which they belong. At the same time, an airport is a miniature metropolis employing thousands of people. Airports are best understood as products of multiple logistical and infrastructural processes of gargantuan scale. Because these forces are similar worldwide, airport buildings tend to resemble each other, prototypes of a building *without qualities*.

Schiphol airport, on the other hand, is one of the new breed of intercontinental gateways and is aligned with the concept of modernity based on the acceleration of information transfer and goods' exchange. Although the nature of the task and the formal language employed resulted in a conventional neo-tech architecture, Schiphol is a vastly more comfortable travel environment than its European counterparts in Paris or London. This achievement is attributed to Benthem Crouwel/NACO's masterplan of 1979 whose combination of commercial acumen and urban potential established a coherent whole from disparate and often conflicting programmatic requirements.

The World Trade Centre (WTC) and Sheraton Hotel are the latest corporate franchises at Schiphol. Sitting above a new parking complex, the office towers sandwich a public corridor that connects them with the central Plaza. While gliding along the conveyor belts the passenger encounters numerous office suites (which are equipped with all the latest telecommunications and can be hired daily), art spaces and water works, all which soothe the nerves of the permanently exhausted global professional. Visitors and executives alike overlook a hypermodern landscape

Amsterdam

Benthem Crouwel Architecten bv/NACO 1989–96

Amsterdam

Benthem Crouwel Architecten bv/NACO 1989–96

through the endless glazed façade. It reveals an architecture that is unemotional, intelligent, and uncommitted. The World Trade Centre does not seek a relationship to its setting, but to the proximity of waiting aircraft and the immediacy of a call on your cellular 'phone.

In comparison with the straight business attitude of the WTC, Schiphol Plaza offers a far more casual atmosphere. Jan Benthem and Mels Crouwel, who originally became involved with the airport when they were commissioned to design a bicycle shed for the employees, conceived a spacious foyer reminiscent of an aircraft hangar. They avoid the confusion of an interior stuffed with retail outlets and snackbars by banning those establishments to a medium-sized mall surrounding the station hall. The vast space is dominated by infoposts and displays whose plain typography guide the way to one of three terminals.

Passengers arriving by train enter the hall from the station below. The discontinuous space of platform and foyer is formidably mediated by a series of slanted travellators which allow a slow transition between levels. This gives the layout a good sense of direction, which also makes the many artworks on permanent display relatively enjoyable. One of my favourite installations is by American artist Jenny Holzer whose 'truisms' are an adequate comment on the superficial ideology of the context. While ascending an escalator that wraps around the vertically suspended LED display, one can read her text messages – for example, 'Protect me from what I want' – that pass up and down at a furious speed.

The international arrival and departure hall above bears the hallmarks of the original terminal buildings from the 1960s: a lucid structure that prioritises orientation and visibility throughout its expanse. An additional countermeasure to prevent disorientation keeps the passenger on the one level, from the check-in counter to boarding the aeroplane, with

Amsterdam

Benthem Crouwel Architecten bv/NACO 1989–96

Benthem Crouwel Architecten bv/NACO 1989–96

a fully glazed airside elevation.

The office slab straddling the landside section of the floating roof houses the administration centres of several airlines based at the airport. In typical Dutch fashion the terminal can handle future extensions: it is made of 50-metre-wide units that can be expanded to a maximum width of 350 metres. If the airport ever outgrows its current location an excavation in the roof parallel to the service core can accommodate a future rail link to a satellite terminal.

Although these qualities are not immediately obvious to passengers, this level of strategic thinking has kept Schiphol from becoming a chaotic mass of mainports such as at JFK in New York or Heathrow in London. By putting consumer satisfaction above overall turnover Schiphol establishes the basic conditions for convenient and efficient air travel. What remains is the uncomfortable thought that even such a benevolent and caring attitude will not challenge the loss of place caused by an airport's transient nature.

ADDRESS Schipholweg 1, Amsterdam
DESIGN TEAM Jan Benthem, Mels Crouwel, Guus Brockmeier, Roelof Gortemaker
CONSULTANTS West 8 Landscape Architects, Branson Coates Architects
CLIENT Amsterdam Airport Schiphol
TRAIN every 15 minutes from Amsterdam Centraal Station
BUS 172 from Amsterdam Centraal Station
CAR motorway A4, A9
ACCESS restricted to public areas

Amsterdam

Benthem Crouwel Architecten bv/NACO 1989–96

Amsterdam

Benthem Crouwel Architecten bv/NACO 1989–96

Noord Holland

VPRO head office, Hilversum 72

Housing, Huizen 78

Teylers Museum extension, Haarlem 80

Zandvoort Circus (amusement centre and cinema) 82

De Hoep visitor centre, Castricum 84

De Realiteit, Almere 86

Library, Zeewolde 88

Museum Nieuwland (polder museum), Lelystad 90

Sportmuseum, Lelystad 92

VPRO head office, Hilversum

Rem Koolhaas hates it. 'It looks like something by OMA, but OMA misunderstood', the big man reportedly said of the work by his former collaborators, who left his office to form MVRDV. Using the initials from their surnames as an eponym in what may be called a post-OMAism, Winy Maas, Jacob van Rijs and Nathalie de Vries are quickly establishing a reputation as the young Turks of Dutch architecture.

VPRO, a private and hugely successful media and broadcasting company that produces unusual programmes, outgrew its former premises. The design of the company's new headquarters was a dream commission for MVRDV who previously were denied their big break when political circumstances prevented the realisation of their competition-winning Europan project for Berlin. The VPRO building, which is mostly office space but has production facilities and a staff restaurant with the best view of Hilversum, thematises the proximity of work and leisure that was one of the client's central concerns. This request along with the repercussions that information technology had on the workplace resulted in a hybrid between the private domain and office environment. MVRDV elaborated the design as an internal landscape that would absorb the stimuli of a hectic office environment as well as the surrounding's lush greenery and have the necessary requisites of communication and privacy.

The effect was achieved by manipulating the concrete floor slab, which was bent, terraced, cut open and wedged until the singular space in-between looked like a distorted version of Le Corbusier's Maison Domino. The continuous interior warps through five levels before arriving on the grass-covered roof. Along the way it disintegrates any notion of spacial hierarchy, axiality and orientation. In spite of breaking such a host of architectural conventions the building obeys directives that define the maximum distance between a workstation and the exterior. To

Noord Holland

MVRDV 1993–97

MVRDV 1993–97

be within the set criteria, the volume is penetrated by a series of courtyards that bring light and air to the central sections. These excavations follow the same strategy as the ground plane, worming their way down through the building. The interplay between the courtyards and deformed floor planes erupts in a breathtaking interior as not seen before.

The architects played with military vocabulary, referring jokingly to the construction phase as 'colonising–clearing–conquering'. Such imagery is strengthened when climbing the slope of the parking lot. At the top, like a fortress with a belly of blue neon tubes, the buildings greet visitors with the curved floor of what appears to be the first level. It turns out to be the third: the main entrance is halfway up the building. The plane of the parking lot slips under the building before it is consumed in a curious loop by the floor above. This gets good grades for looks but, even better, it destroys any concept of above/below and inside/outside. This attitude of flexible uncertainty stems from the first idea for the façade:

Winy Maas In the VPRO building we tried originally to avoid the façade. We wanted to use only these kind of megastore heaters so that birds could freely enter and you have only a difference in temperature between in- and outside. No walls. That was the main interest. I see you are puzzled.

KB What about when it rains?

WM Rain is not a problem. The issue is safety – how to deal with that. Another issue is still energy costs. In the project we are working on now, we are pushing the idea by inserting three windmills inside the building so it becomes a kind of turbo office. So then you have free energy.

Although the truth behind the proposal must lie between hyperbole and

Noord Holland

MVRDV 1993–97

the lack of resources actually to design the façade at that time, Maas eventually came up with an equally appeasing concept. In a painstaking research phase the office calculated the percentage of daylight and the resulting heat emissions of all sides. According to the collected data, sheets of (1) deep green insulated-glass, (2) blueish mirrored-glass and (3) clear glass were selected to fulfil the customised performance criteria. The façade's eclectic appearance is testimony to the constantly searching minds of its creators. Barely escaping the authority of their mentor Koolhaas, whose formal vocabulary they use deliberately, Maas, Van Rijs and De Vries are already defining their architecture by an unprejudiced amount of statistical information. The VPRO building is certainly one of the most significant projects built in the 1990s in The Netherlands. It is also witness to the unrewarded brilliance of Koolhaas who prepared the ground for his former disciples.

Noord Holland

ADDRESS Sumatralaan 45, Hilversum
DESIGN TEAM Jacob van Rijs, Winy Maas, Nathalie de Vries, Stefan Witteman, Alex Brouwer, Arjan Mulder, Willem Timmer, Joost Glissener
CLIENT VPRO Hilversum
FLOOR AREA 10,000 square metres
GETTING THERE 5-minute walk from Hilversum Noord station
ACCESS only to perimeter

MVRDV 1993–97

Noord Holland

MVRDV 1993–97

Housing, Huizen

Neutelings Riedijk Architects are never short of an idea for a new apartment typology and demonstrate the ability once more in Huizen, a wealthy suburb of Hilversum. Commissioned to draw the masterplan for the shore area of the Gooimeer, they developed a set of terraced houses that exploit the view over the expansive water. The restriction of the 6-metre-wide plots was a problem for the panoramic houses the architects originally imagined. Cleverly, they rotated the orientation of the living/kitchen area of two neighbouring houses by 90° so that they overlapped giving a 12-metre-wide bay window to each dwelling unit. The houses, which are separate, stack their living rooms above each other, from where there are exceptional views over Het Gooi.

Because of the houses' intertwined property line they are legally defined as apartments – even though each property boasts a car port and a garden at the back. This potentially negative selling point was not a problem because purchasers were paying for the privilege of the fantastic view.

ADDRESS Hardwijkerzand, Huizen
DESIGN TEAM Willem Jan Neutelings (PROJECT ARCHITECT), Michiel Riedijk, Willem Bruijn, Gerrit Schilder
CLIENT Bouwfonds Woningbouw bv, Haarlem
BUS 135 from Hilversum Noord station to Stadspark, then a 10-minute walk
ACCESS public areas only

Noord Holland

Neutelings Riedijk Architecten bv 1994–96

Neutelings Riedijk Architecten bv 1994–96

Teylers Museum extension, Haarlem

The Teylers Museum is reminiscent of the Egyptian Museum in Cairo – a dusty old institution, with plenty of charm and a dose of faded grandeur. It is located in the inner city of the chocolate-box town of Haarlem and its imposing façade looks over the Spaarne river.

Not surprisingly, the first museum ever built in The Netherlands needed an extension to accommodate the rising number of visitors. When an open competition was staged, the museum received an enormous amount of entries. Hubert-Jan Henket, the architect responsible for the extension to the Boimans van Beuningen Museum in Rotterdam (see page 248), won the commission with a design that respected the issues connected with the complicated site. Set in a park adjacent to a private block, the extension connects the old museum with the Zegelwaarden without disrupting the lives of people around the park.

As the original museum is entirely lit by daylight and closes at dusk, Henket's extension is set away from the building to avoid casting a shadow on it. Clad in glass panels with aluminium blinds above, light entering the extension can easily be controlled. The window details of wood and brass are reminiscent of the mechanical instruments, microscopes and barometers on display in the museum. In fact, the new components accentuate the beauty of the museum and do not overshadow it.

ADDRESS Spaarne 16, Haarlem
PROJECT ARCHITECTS Hubert-Jan Henket, Henk van Laarhoven, Teresa van Rosmalen, Jan Veldman
LANDSCAPE ARCHITECT Buys en Van der Wijst Interieur
CLIENT Stichting tot Steun aan Culturele Instellingen
GETTING THERE 5-minute walk from Haarlem station
ACCESS open

Noord Holland

Hubert-Jan Henket Architecten bv 1992–96

Noord Holland

Hubert-Jan Henket Architecten bv 1992–96

Zandvoort Circus (amusement centre and cinema)

FM Zandvoort Circus is the most exuberant building in Holland but at the same time the most banal programme and banal place.

Sjoerd Soeters Yes, Zandvoort is the most ordinary seaside, it's like the Brighton of Holland, so it's a joke in a way; to say Zandvoort is so completely kitsch. And the idea of the flags is to mark sections of Zandvoort, to show the beauty committee what they are meant to do. If you order an ice cream you get the flag on top as well. And the Dutch flag is a symbol for our coast.

KB It seems to lack a certain pretentiousness.

SS Yes, the pretentiousness of my colleagues. Dutch architects are so pretentious about the neo, and they make such dull buildings.

KB The programme could be anywhere.

SS The idea of the client was that he didn't want to have a dark atmosphere like most arcades are because he wanted to have a very wide public … the whole family. We made different emotional environments for the two types of users: the elderly ladies are on the top floor where we have a blue carpet, and an open view. So for the boys out at night we developed a theory about going back to the womb so we have a red carpet in the middle of all apparatus around you shouting and talking to you. And in retrospect it has been very successful, it worked very well.

ADDRESS Gasthuisplein 1, Zandvoort
PROJECT ARCHITECT Sjoerd Soeters
GETTING THERE 3-minute walk from Zandvoort station
CLIENT Play In bv
ACCESS open

Noord Holland

Architectenbureau Soeters 1986–91

Architectenbureau Soeters 1986–91

De Hoep visitor centre, Castricum

Situated in a national reserve on the outskirts of Castricum, the De Hoep visitor centre has a pop science exhibition that tells of the cycle of water in this protected environment.

The landscaped building assimilates the sand dunes of the seafront nearby. Surging from the ground like a wave, the curve of the roof reaches its climax above the foyer. The top layer is planted with moss and beach grass held in place by chicken wire and the fully glazed elevations seemingly make this layer float above the ground. Large, concrete tubes, similar to those for sewage systems, lead into the building and set the theme. They intersect a dune, over which the building sweeps gracefully. This cloaks the changing space of the interior, while from the outside De Hoep gives the impression of being a single-storey structure of constant height. A conical lecture theatre dominating the central hall pokes through the roof. Its distorted plane was achieved with a timber beam structure that adapts to the gentle curves prescribed by the dunes. The constraints of the limited budget are neutralised by such resourcefulness.

Noord Holland

ADDRESS Zeeweg, Castricum
DESIGN TEAM Maarten Min
CLIENT P W N, Bloemendaal
GETTING THERE 10-minute bicycle ride from Castricum station
ACCESS open; entrance fee

Min 2 Produkties 1992

Noord Holland

Min 2 Produkties 1992

De Realiteit, Almere

The garden city of Almere is a refuge for commuters from the urban chaos of Amsterdam. On the edge of Almere is de Realiteit, a small neighbourhood of experimental but functional homes by young architects and constructed with small budgets. The use of industrial materials in most of the homes keeps costs low and lends the settlement a spartan and somewhat idealistic feel.

One dwelling is entirely of cargo containers stacked like matchsticks and joined lengthwise which results in an essentially vertical composition with a small footprint. A cute container-garage adds to the humour of the site, while the fire engine red of the house screams exuberance and adds to the monumentality of the structure. An ultimate DIY dream, the success of the design is completely based on the inventiveness of the architects.

Across the lane Teun Koolhaas has designed a house suspended on stilts, a feature influenced by Japanese design. Instead of focusing on an idyllic garden, as most suburban houses do, Koolhaas consciously acknowledges the view of Amsterdam in the distance. A few steps give access to a fabulous winter garden where a steel ship-staircase leads to the living areas on the first floor.

Noord Holland

ADDRESS Realiteit 7, Almere
PROJECT ARCHITECT Teun Koolhaas
CLIENT bv Ontwerpbureau ir. Teun Koolhaas Associates
BUS 1, 3, 4, 215 to Haringvlietstraat
ACCESS visitors' parcourse with inscriptions and information

Teun Koolhaas Associates 1985–89

Noord Holland

Teun Koolhaas Associates 1985–89

Library, Zeewolde

The library at Zeewolde is unintentionally beautiful. It could be described as architecture in its most archaic form. The concrete carcass rests on twisted stilts that seem to bend under the load, and no element is employed by Koen van Velsen in a premeditated fashion. Although there are many windows and openings, their position and arrangement do not suggest they are there to be looked out from, but rather their presence is necessitated by a inconceivable quality of the building. They have lost all their functional meaning and as one goes to the first floor they participate in the structure's disintegration into thin air. The library's coarse simplicity is as striking as one of van Velsen's few statements on his buildings: 'There is nothing one can say about architecture'.

ADDRESS Kerkstraat 2, Zeewolde, Flevoland
CLIENT Gemeente Zeewolde
CAR motorway A6 to Zeewolde
BUS 159 from Almere station
ACCESS open

Noord Holland

Architectenburo Koen van Velsen 1985–89

Architectenburo Koen van Velsen 1985–89

Museum Nieuwland (polder museum), Lelystad

Visiting Polders is like revisiting the recent past. Land reclaimed from the North Sea was only habitable years after the laborious work was done, and the city planners of the 1950s and 1960s created entire towns that now feel plastic, cold and inorganic. Cultural stimulation was the last point on the agenda. However, in Lelystad a museum-park has been developed on the outskirts of town. It is here that Victor Mani's Sportmuseum (page 92) neighbours a new museum dedicated to history of the Polders.

Of ten architects, the clients made a shortlist of three and had Benthem Crouwel as first choice. There was a very small budget and a strict brief: the building was to be an information centre and museum. Daylight was also limited to conserve sensitive documents. Benthem Crouwel, therefore, designed a tubular-shaped building suspended above ground level by a plinth which mimics a section of a dyke.

The entrance, at ground level, leads to a reception/shop area. A visitor then unceremoniously enters the museum, choosing either to see the exhibition on the floors above or visit the café which looks out to sea. Because natural light enters the building from either end, fragile exhibits are shown in the darker areas located in the middle of the tube. The materials are inexpensive, except for the giant wooden beams used to support the structure, which were felled from the rainforest. The exhibition design is fun, with interactive elements that appeal to children and adults alike.

ADDRESS Oostvaardersdijk, Lelystad
PROJECT ARCHITECT Ton Liemburg
BUS 150 from Lelystad station
ACCESS open

Noord Holland

Benthem Crouwel Architecten bv 1991–94

Noord Holland

Benthem Crouwel Architecten bv 1991–94

Sportmuseum, Lelystad

When the Sportsmuseum decided to build on a new site, Rem Koolhaas (who was commissioned to do the original design which was abandoned because of lack of money) was unavailable and suggested that the job be given to one of his underlings, Victor Mani. Like all of Rem's disciples who are at the forefront of architecture in The Netherlands, Mani tests unconventional means of building which at times do not meet the client's expectations.

Owing to a tight budget, the building is only one-third of the proposed scheme. The north façade will be expanded upon to accommodate a basketball court/arena. The 600-square-metre glass wall of the south façade would bake visitors were it not for the specially designed polyester corrugated panels. Originally meant to be fastened with Velcro, the panels are now held by bolts to protect them from the fierce polder winds.

Entering the building on the western side, visitors encounter the reception area and can watch sports clips on screen. The rest of the ground floor is a large, open space punctuated by a wedge-shaped ramp that was a consequence of the lack of funds available for flattening the dyke. Unlike this display of resourcefulness, Mani insisted on integrating six adjacent doors, which create a wind-tunnel effect when the entrance is opened. The modern concrete aesthetic of the ground floor contrasts with the wooden nostalgia of the first floor, where an Olympic exhibition leads to a café that spills out on an outdoor terrace. Overall the building has some brilliant moments and is a must-see for the sports *aficionado*.

ADDRESS Museumweg 10, Lelystad
CLIENT Stichting Gebouw Nederlands Sportmuseum/Lelystad
BUS 150 from Lelystad station
ACCESS open

Noord Holland

Architectenburo Victor Mani 1993–96

Architectenburo Victor Mani 1993–96

Groningen and Friesland

Groninger Museum 96

De Hunze boathouse, Groningen 102

Toilet, Groningen 104

Shops, apartments and offices, Waagstraat, Groningen 106

Public Library, Groningen 108

Rode Weeshuisstraat housing, Groningen 110

Apartment tower, Laan Corpus den Hoorn, Groningen 112

Landsteinerlaan housing, Groningen 114

GasUnie Building, Groningen 116

'Vos Maupertus' interior design superstore, Groningen 120

Bjoeks climbing hall, Groningen 122

Fries Museum, Leeuwarden 124

Stadsschouwburg De Harmonie, Leeuwarden 126

The ugliest house in The Netherlands, Leeuwarden 128

Groninger Museum

Immediately on leaving the NS station in Groningen, visitors are confronted by the sight of the unusual, colourful and hulking mass of buildings that comprise the Groninger Museum. In 1987, after nearly 10 years of discussion, it was decided that the museum would move out of its old premises on the Praediniussingel to a new location. The city and province of Groningen agreed to the construction of a new museum on the condition that a third party would provide a substantial part of the funding. Such sponsorship was given by Nederlandse Gasunie (Dutch Gas) in celebration of its 25th anniversary.

After much consideration the Zwaaikom was chosen as the new site because of its central location and ideological position as a gateway between the old and new parts of the city. Straddling the Verbindings-kanaal, the museum separates Central Station from the nineteenth-century canal and simultaneously forms a bridge for pedestrians and cyclists connecting the rail and bus stations with the inner city.

The design of the building needed to reflect the diversity of the museum's collections, which range from ancient to modern times, and from Eastern to Western styles. From the beginning the four pavilions would be designed, inside and outside, by different architects working under the guidance of Alessandro Mendini. Mendini had never built a museum before, but it was important that he had experience coordinating the work of others. He is responsible for the gleaming gold tower that dominates the scheme and which forms the central point of the floorplan. It is based on a gasometer and is used for offices and storage, and serves as the main entrance to the museum. Juxtaposed with this essentially vertical structure are two low-rise buildings in pastel pink and green, also designed by Mendini. It is here that the staff entrance is located, as well as the bookshop and an exuberant café, complete with Alessi table acces-

Atelier Mendini with Team 4 Architecten 1988–92

Atelier Mendini with Team 4 Architecten 1988–92

sories such as ashtrays and salt and pepper shakers. To the east and west of the central cluster lie pavilions connected by a semi-underwater corridor that doubles as exhibition space. A red brick pavilion designed by Michele de Lucchi forms the base of the western section and houses the archaeological and historical collection. The use of brick as an exterior material is a reflection on the characteristics of the historic inner city. Resting above this is the aluminium cylindrical pavilion – its interior designed by Philippe Starck – that holds the decorative arts collection, which includes 8000 pieces of Oriental ceramics. The stark contrast between the exterior of the pavilions is echoed in their interiors – de Lucchi's exhibition halls are dark affairs with specially designed, mirrored, one-source lighting (designed by Roberto Ostinelli) that dramatises the objects. With similar flair but a more ethereal aesthetic, Starck uses white chiffon curtains to formulate false walls in what is essentially a large, open circular space.

The lower part of the eastern cluster, also designed by Mendini, is used for temporary exhibitions. The wonderfully saturated colours of the gallery rooms here were selected by Dutch artist Peter Struycken. Above this lies the roof pavilion, designed by Coop Himmelb(l)au: the twisted, exploded shape seems to promise a new approach to architecture. Unfortunately, the Viennese architects exhaust all their talents on the façade leaving little for the blank interior, which radiates the spatial tension of a garage. Inconsistencies between the dynamic exterior and the straightforward linear interior are hastily glossed over by a number of gimmicks that confuse radical chic with design talent. For example, to view certain seventeenth-century paintings hung from the ceiling, the visitor has to walk along a suspended steel bridge.

An enormously ambitious and expensive project, the museum repre-

Atelier Mendini with Team 4 Architecten 1988–92

Ateller Mendini with Team 4 Architecten 1988–92

sents, once again, Groningen's progressive attitude towards contemporary architecture. The dizzying effects question traditional notions of museum design and the limits of good taste. With its fetishisation of design and its histrionic presence, the building is more than a museum, becoming the postmodern ideal of the museum as a utopian cathedral – that is, the centre point and symbol of a city that can educate and amuse in equal measure.

ADDRESS Museumeiland 1, Groningen
DESIGN TEAM Alessandro Mendini, Francesco Mendini, Gerard Schijf with Philippe Starck, Michele de Lucchi, Coop Himmelb(l)au
CONSULTANTS Ingenieursburo Wassenaar, Haren
CLIENT Gemeente Groningen
BUDGET NFL30 million
BUS 1–7, 9, 13, 15 to Groningen station
ACCESS open; entrance fee

Atelier Mendini with Team 4 Architecten 1988–92

Atelier Mendini with Team 4 Architecten 1988–92

De Hunze boathouse, Groningen

When the city municipality decided to place the Groninger Museum on the Verbindingskanal (page 96), the De Hunze Rowing Club also had to move premises to a site it had originally inhabited in the nineteenth century. The club had a 130-year-long tradition to consider and needed an architect who could synthesise the tension between the medieval and modern elements of the spectacular location, sited at the junction of two inner-city canals.

As the roof slopes gently up from the street, the boathouse literally turns its back to the land, focusing on the water. The plan reveals a play on the geometry of a repeating equilateral triangle that knits the street, social spaces and boats with the water. The arrangement of functions is simple and effective: bicycle stands, café and terrace are above the storage and workshop areas where the boats are maintained. A thin, triangular pier floats in front of the storage area, thus maximising the length of its lateral side and allowing an eight to moor alongside. It incorporates the transition from the solid to the fluid in a modest, but lyrical, manner.

Although the only minimal thing about the building is its budget, it achieves spatial beauty. The sober arrangement of unfinished concrete structure, glass panels, oaken cladding and grating establishes a coherent visual code that makes clear the working elements in the overall composition. Daan's exploration of traditional architectural craftsmanship does not deny the contemporary attitude that is so prevalent in this project.

ADDRESS Raedinussingel, Groningen
CLIENT K G R De Hunze
DESIGN TEAM Anoul Bouwman
BUS 1, 3, 4, 5, 13, 15 to Emmaplein
ACCESS open

Gunnar Daan 1989–92

Gunnar Daan 1989–92

Toilet, Groningen

This project is a permanent fixture from 'A Star is Born', a 7-week festival held in Groningen in 1996 in which various locations provided discourses on public spaces that took the form of stage, accommodation, travel and toilet. The importance of such a festival cannot be underestimated: not only does it serve to inform the public about the changing shape of their city, it also attracts visitors from surrounding areas and helps to place the city firmly in one's mental map.

The toilet was designed by Rem Koolhaas and Gro Bonesmo from OMA in collaboration with Erwin Olaf, a commercial and fine-art photographer, and is located on a public square that includes an outdoor café. The exterior mural by Olaf depicts the battle of the sexes. Olaf, who is known for his controversial images, attempted to exercise some modesty in this public commission. The interior, also covered with his images, has simple aluminium unisex facilities. The structure is covered by a roof with a collage by OMA concerning the global village.

In the guide book accompanying the festival, the critic Bart Lootsma notes that public and private, masculine and feminine, architecture and art, high and low culture come together in this simple but powerful piece. One of two permanent projects from the festival, and now an indispensable part of the square's character, the toilet marks Groningen's progressive attitude to architecture and its ability to mix pleasure with practicality.

ADDRESS Reimakersrijge, Groningen
PROJECT ARCHITECTS Rem Koolhaas, Gro Bonesmo
CLIENT Gemeente Groningen
BUS 1, 3–5, 13, 15 to Emmaplein
ACCESS open

Office for Metropolitan Architecture and Erwin Olaf 1995–96

Office for Metropolitan Architecture and Erwin Olaf 1995–96

Shops, apartments and offices, Waagstraat, Groningen

Dissatisfied with the postwar extension to the town hall on the Grote Markt, Groningen city council ordered its demolition and commissioned a new infill on one of their most important public squares. Natalini Architetti's proposal was chosen from a shortlist of firms whose brief was to define the sensitive threshold between Grote Markt and Vismarkt.

Two design themes are prevalent: the public characteristics are deemed more important than a historically correct reconstruction of the prewar situation; and Groningen's medieval morphology is formally referred to. The new ensemble consists of two blocks along Guldenstraat and Waagstraat and, perpendicular to them, a third, slightly curved block on the northern edge of Grote Markt. Given the need for retail space on the ground floor, with housing and offices above, the outcome is formally cohesive although the typologies are not that inventive. Idiosyncratic pitched roofs, precast concrete elements and sandstone cladding are used to assimilate with the surroundings. This project is thus one of many to treat the inner cities as museums, articulating little other than a programme based in consumption.

Paradoxically, or perhaps in recognition of the loss of public space as a forum for individual expression, the city council also organised the urban festival 'A Star is Born' (see page 104) to reintroduce the notion of *civitas*, an ideology that Natalini's project fails to achieve.

ADDRESS Waagstraat, Guldenstraat, Grote Markt Noordzijde
DESIGN TEAM Adolfo Natalini, Marco Magni, Gaetano Martella, Nazario Scelsi, Corinne Schrauwen
BUS 1, 2, 3, 6, 11 to Centrum
ACCESS open

Groningen and Friesland

Natalini Architetti 1991–96

Natalini Architetti 1991–96

Public Library, Groningen

In addition to the widely acclaimed Groninger Museum (see page 96), the city boasts another work by an internationally renowned architect: Giorgio Grassi's Public Library. True to his belief that architecture should be comprehensible to the general public, the design restrains from façade gymnastics and follows the typologies of the street in which it is located.

Enclosing a recessed courtyard, the library consists of two undecorated brick blocks that replicate the proportions and rhythm set by the neighbouring mansions. The chameleon-like *Gestalt* goes as far as repeating the number of windows per floor that face the street. While this insistence on continuing the grown urban fabric stems from a historical reading, it also refuses to be monumental. Thus it is not entirely clear where the public function becomes manifest. Apart from the modest street elevation and the entrance set back in the narrow courtyard, there are little clues to be found inside.

The many functions of the building include the Leescafé, where books and coffee combine pleasurably, and the mediatheque and children's library. The programmatic impact of the elements materialises neither in the floorplans nor in the spatial organisation. The circulation does not even seek to create a transition from the public realm to the study areas. Although the library does not seem to command a big budget, the bland interior with its standard details and the use of off-the-shelf materials stands out oddly from the skilful exterior composition.

ADDRESS Oude Boteringestraat 18, Groningen
CLIENT PGGM, Zeist/Mabon Inc., Rijswijk
BUS 3, 4, 5, 15 to Emmaplein
ACCESS open

Giorgio Grassi 1989–92

Giorgio Grassi 1989–92

Rode Weeshuisstraat housing, Groningen

In a rare opportunity this infill accounts for the medieval fabric of Groningen's old town and re-establishes the design of a former orphanage's cloister garden. The combination of a renovated courtyard house of the sixteenth century with a modern apartment building for senior citizens creates an urban environment based firmly in its historic function.

The architecture is not overt and works to differentiate the public and collective spheres. Light strips of white and grey masonry and large window panels reflect the open and participatory mood of the courtyard, while the introverted red-brick exterior secludes the block from the buzz of the city centre. All the second-floor apartments are reached by central stairs. The third-floor maisonettes are slightly recessed from the inner perimeter by a gangway. The squeezed floorplans are compensated for by high ceilings, indulging the views over Groningen's roofscape.

An informal passage runs to the northern perimeter of the old town via the semiprivate courtyards. After five o'clock the gate that separates visitors from the inhabitants shuts and permission is needed to enter the sanctum. We looked around with a resident who emphasised the privacy of the place and explained how concerts for the general public were held in the courtyard during the summer. In this way the building is more than a calm enclave in the city centre for the lucky few, but an asset shared with fellow citizens.

ADDRESS Rode Weeshuisstraat, Groningen
DESIGN TEAM Cees Nagelkerke, Willem van Seumern, Lilian Korver
SIZE 33 subsidised rental apartments
BUS 1, 2, 3, 6, 11 to Centrum
ACCESS daily 9.00–17.00

Architectenbureau Nagelkerke 1990–93

Architectenbureau Nagelkerke 1990–93

Apartment tower, Laan Corpus den Hoorn, Groningen

The tall apartment building has made a remarkable comeback in The Netherlands during the past ten years. The monofunctional ideology of the 1960s is being reinvented and repackaged as 'good' – aestheticised high-rises. In Corpus den Hoorn, a mostly low-rise area of Groningen, a 14-storey tower works as a landmark, elevating the district from its urban backwater character.

Internal organisation is expressed in a trapezoidal plan of two mirrored apartments of two-to-three bedrooms. Vertically arranged into three separate volumes, the narrow backside contains the smaller apartment type, as well as the core for elevator and staircase. Here the balconies have been subordinated to the volumetric closure of the block and are glazed winter gardens. The western façade facing Corpus den Hoorn is accentuated by balconies in horizontal strips. The use of corrugated steel on the shorter sides of the block was dictated by the low budget. Enhanced by the window grid, the façade's hermetic appearance is only counterbalanced by pastel-coloured rectangles that break up the large surface.

This concentrated appearance is emblematic of Claus and Kaan's aversion to fussy detailing, an attitude that seems unfashionable at a time when architecture as a means of cultural expression is losing its significance. Nevertheless, they constantly refine the design until they achieve a precision in tune with the original concept. It is this contemplation and control over the design process that highlights their work.

ADDRESS Laan Corpus den Hoorn, Groningen
DESIGN TEAM Felix Claus, Cees Kaan, Ronald Rientjes
BUS 6, 52 to Laan Corpus den Hoorn
ACCESS none

Groningen and Friesland

Claus en Kaan Architecten 1995–97

Claus en Kaan Architecten 1995–97

Landsteinerlaan housing, Groningen

This unassuming housing estate uses the opposites of open and closed spaces, and of hard edges between public and private domains. It establishes a far more sophisticated system of relations than would initially be expected. Interlocking a communal green, a row of townhouses facing three mid-rise apartment blocks form the V-shaped layout.

Cees Kaan We started with one building, because that was what the city council wanted. On an urban-design level, we felt that this was not the right scale, it should be broken down, it should be three buildings. We found that the intermediate spaces – we struggled a long time with them – if we could turn them inside out, if you did not look any longer at the buildings, see these spaces, you could read them differently: the buildings are not important, they are simply an in-fill between spaces.

Unfortunately, as the defined volumes are too large to be experienced from street level, Kaan's ideas are not evident, although the same strategy works well with the smaller townhouses. The geometric simplicity stems from the architect's obsession with the abstract appearance of surfaces. Painstakingly avoiding any symbolic content, all façades use different materials that accentuate the plasticity of the building volumes. Their considered planes give little clue to what lies behind, but help to transform the area by night when the fully glazed access galleries turn the blocks into a neon-bathed streetscape, more attune with a hard urban reality than the cosiness of Landsteinerlaan.

ADDRESS Landsteinerlaan, Donderslaan, Groningen
BUS 6 to Corpus den Hoorn
ACCESS none

Claus en Kaan Architecten 1991–93

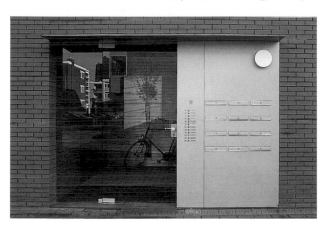

Claus en Kaan Architecten 1991–93

GasUnie Building, Groningen

When Nederlandse GasUnie had outgrown their premises they opted to rebuild and chose Ton Alberts and Max van Huut unanimously from a group of invited practices. The architects created an organic architecture in every facet of design and believe that the rectangular arrangements of modernism inhibit creativity and communication among users: accordingly all surfaces in the building – walls, staircases, even desks – are 4.5° off perpendicular.

Alberts and van Huut's 18-storey building is an imposing structure that dominates the generally low-rise skyline of Groningen. Set beside a park on the southern outskirts of the city, its striking external features include a pattern of tonal bricks and an impressive cascade of blue glass that the company refers to as 'the waterfall'. It is set off from the street, which is a main thoroughfare, by a small moat filled with water. Recognising the needs of cyclists, who rule the streets of Groningen, the architects designed bicycle sheds cleverly landscaped into the piazza before the main entrance.

Once inside, the entry hall leads into a fantastic glass-enclosed atrium with a freely suspended, 16-storey spiral staircase which subtly changes colour as it rises. This 'vertical garden' sets a peaceful tone for the rest of the building. The ground floor has public utilities: reception, meeting rooms, library, an auditorium for 200 people and an area for temporary art exhibitions. Art is featured heavily in the building, and seems to exceed the 1 per cent-allocation-of-budget rule in The Netherlands.

Communication was the principal idea in Nederlandse GasUnie's brief for the new building: in their old premises staff from different departments communicated only by telephone. The programme's preoccupation with social spaces is pervasive. Similar to office regulations in Anglo-Saxon countries, the only smoking area in the building is the café and

Architectenbureau Alberts & van Huut 1989–94

Architectenbureau Alberts & van Huut 1989–94

bar on the first floor. This policy not only ensures fresh air in the work-place; it also provides staff with a 'habitual' meeting point. Each floor has a central area for the collection of post to encourage casual contact between employees of different departments. Also, by placing the call buttons for the elevators on freestanding sculptural plinths outside the lift shafts, the architects seem to invite workers to observe passers-by and the atrium below.

ADDRESS Concourslaan 17, Groningen
LANDSCAPE ARCHITECT Jörn Copijn/
Copijn Groenadviseurs Utrecht
FLOOR AREA 45,000 square metres
BUS 6 to Martinihal
ACCESS once a year in September on a
prearranged visitors' day

Architectenbureau Alberts & van Huut 1989–94

Architectenbureau Alberts & van Huut 1989–94

'Vos Maupertus' interior design superstore, Groningen

For architectural buffs, the Vos Maupertus interior design store could easily be dismissed were it not for its curious lingering on the threshold between industrial kitsch and shopping theme park.

The exquisite cadaver of three juxtaposed volumes of the complex holds the various operations of the company, which range from a furniture and housewares department, their interior design consultancy to an art gallery and brasserie. Although the building radiates a tremendous self-confidence, its front is unfocused: should it address the street or the motorway? The plethora of shapes and types, which seem to borrow from everyone from OMA to Koen van Velsen, are employed for no discernable reason except effect. A lot of attention has been given to the diversification of the architectural types such as the atrium, terrace and courtyard, while the presence of so much benevolence suffocates a coherent solution. Everything looks well done, yet feels wrong. For example, the approach from the back of the building passes under an elevated depot before reaching the entrance by way of a roofed vestibule next to the motorway.

Despite the flaws, even such an ill-disciplined building is entertaining. It is much more blissful than the average museum of applied arts as everything on display is for sale. The vast collection of designer gadgets and furniture add to the theatrical qualities, making it an enjoyable sightseeing and shopping trip.

ADDRESS Laan Corpus den Hoorn 100, Groningen
DESIGN TEAM Bart van Borselen Vos, Roderick Vos, Claire Teeuwen
CONSULTANTS Ingo Maurer, Philippe Starck
BUS 6
ACCESS open

Groningen and Friesland

Otonomo Architecten 1996

Otonomo Architecten 1996

Bjoeks climbing hall, Groningen

The speedy process of suburbanisation and the correlating increase in leisure time have profoundly changed the look of city expansions in The Netherlands. Large park-and-ride schemes encourage commuters to take public transport to work, and, despite the low density of the average suburban setting, these transferia become nodes that include leisure, shopping and recreational functions. They condense what one could consider as the nuclei of a new local community. A development of sports facilities in conjunction with a transferium forms a typical pattern exploiting activities not possible in the claustrophobic spaces of inner cities. One example of this phenomenon is a transferium in Noorddijk in north-east Groningen.

Next to Karelse van der Meer's indoor sportspark and ice-skating rink, separated by the expanse of the parking lot, are the jumbled volumes of Johannes Moehrlein's climbing hall, aptly called 'Bjoeks' (boulders). Two cubes are rotated and intersected to create a multifaceted interior that offers participants varying degrees of climbing difficulty. The programme and structure blend as the tapestry of artificial grips and holes dissolve the usual notions of wall and ceiling. Visitors can watch the action from the café opposite the climbing faces. On the exterior the entrance and café terrace clash awkwardly with the pure dynamics of the tilted structure. By aestheticising the straightforward parts of the brief and dealing with them separately from the industrial-shed aesthetic, the building loses some of its casual blandness.

ADDRESS Bieskemaar 3, Groningen
CLIENT OSW Gemeente Groningen
BUS 3, 4, 6, 9, 10
ACCESS open

Johannes Moehrlein 1996

Johannes Moehrlein 1996

Fries Museum, Leeuwarden

The original Fries Museum was in the eighteenth-century Eysingahuis. The local government decided that the Resistance Museum (dedicated to documenting opposition to the Nazi occupation) would be a part of the Fries Museum. This, combined with the need to exhibit modern art and the ever-increasing collection, prompted an architectural solution.

Rather than a competition, museum and government officials consulted other experts to choose an architect. The client wanted to use as much local resources as possible, but without compromising quality. Gunnar Daan was selected for his Frisian heritage as well as his first-hand knowledge of the museum, having been involved with projects there in the past.

Daan's brief included three major tasks: to renovate the existing museum, to design an entrance hall and connection between the two buildings, and to renew the old display cases. A scheme involving a suspended pedestrian bridge was denounced by the community, which resulted in an underground tunnel that cost three times as much. The opposing façades of the new sites contain triangular window motifs in the centre of a pattern of slate-grey panels that are a metre square. Each year a different artist is commissioned to design a panel. It is intended that after a few years a hieroglyphic effect will result. Sculptures of a goat on an egg and seven ravens that adorn the roofs of these sections are by Dutch artists Tilly Buy and Gerard Groenewoud.

ADDRESS Turfmarkt 11, Leeuwarden
CLIENT Stichting 'De Kanselarij', Leeuwarden
COST NFL22 million
GETTING THERE 5-minute walk from Leeuwarden station
ACCESS open; entrance fee

Gunnar Daan 1992–93

Groningen and Friesland

Gunnar Daan 1992–93

Stadsschouwburg De Harmonie, Leeuwarden

This recently finished theatre on the edge of Leeuwarden's medieval centre is, justifiably, the city's pride and joy. After decades of alterations and reconstruction, the old venue was in a state of congestion that defeated any attempt at modernisation. A winning competition entry by De Architecten Cie/Frits van Dongen displayed the most feasible concept for the available land. The spatial constraints meant that the areas are organised in strips parallel to the building's axis. Auditoria and stage houses form a stacked ensemble in a large, unifying glass skin that swishes dynamically towards the nearby canal.

Public areas such as foyers, bars and restaurants are in full view of the road. On each side staircases slice through the vertical expanse between the external walls and the perimeter of the auditoria. The other non-descript elevation houses administrative and service functions, including the theatre's most impressive gadget, a 25-ton-capacity elevator that can lift entire trucks to the second floor.

Coded in black, red and gold, the interiors are atmospheric, a feeling only surpassed by the mirrored toilets. The vivid colours and floating ellipsoids echo OMA's Dance Theatre in The Hague. The most obvious discrepancy, though, is that the design does not use the spatial complexity to the full: the linear, box-like arrangement of the public functions leaves the potential of the ceiling's claustrophobic decline under the seating areas untouched.

ADDRESS Ruiterskwartier 4, Leeuwarden
CLIENT Gemeente Leeuwarden
BUS 5
ACCESS open

De Architecten Cie/Frits van Dongen 1990–94

Groningen and Friesland

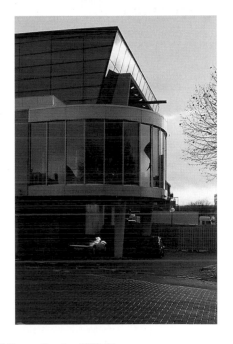

De Architecten Cie/Frits van Dongen 1990–94

The ugliest house in The Netherlands, Leeuwarden

Max., a rising talent from Rotterdam, had their first commission in Leeuwarden. In its contrast to the suburban surroundings the house struck me as being the victim in Kafka's *Metamorphosis*.

Rients Dijkstra Some aspects of the house I like a lot, other parts I hate. It is not for nothing that you mainly find pictures of the street elevation, which is much more successful than the garden side. The average suburban Dutch house has all these characteristics: little crossbars in the window, thatched roof, whitewashed walls. When the clients approached us with 'we want to have the house like this, can you do a good floor plan? Help us avoid mistakes', we said, 'well, why don't you come and look at this project and this material and have you ever seen this?' By and by they went with the design, which in itself was not radical, but radical compared with the point of departure.

FM There is a certain heroic attitude to it.

RD They very much enjoy the house. Every time I see them they congratulate me on the fact that the house works so well. At the same time almost everyone in the neighbourhood loathes it, which is why it was called the ugliest house in Holland in the press. It seems that only children like it. Somehow this does not annoy the owners … After they stopped wanting the average, their confidence was boosted by having something out of the ordinary, which I think is great.

ADDRESS Okkingastate 6, Leeuwarden
DESIGN TEAM Rients Dijkstra, Rianne Makkink, Mark Schendel
BUS 2 to Schierstins
ACCESS none

Groningen and Friesland

Max. Architectuur Stedenbouw 1992–93

Groningen and Friesland

Max. Architectuur Stedenbouw 1992–93

Overijssel

Public Library, Almelo   132
Rijksmuseum Twenthe, Enschede   134

Public Library, Almelo

A public library in the small town of Almelo is another fine project from the prolific Mecanoo Architects. Designed in the first half of the 1990s when the firm included the young Dutch architects of the moment, the library employs their trademarks of an exquisite attention to detail and a sumptuous juxtaposition of materials and colour.

The prestigious location, close to the town hall (J J P Oud's last building, 1963), was determined by the council's ambitions. Their long-term urban policy meant that the building had to address the post-industrial vacuum left in the city centre. Combining distressed copper cladding, ultramarine glass panels and impressive, double-height windows with a fragmented architectural expression, the building challenges the context of Oud's project across the street.

Such an effort has not gone unnoticed by the public, and their endorsement is shown in the library's popularity. On the ground floor are the most sought-after departments, exhibition cases for new books, and an inexpensive café with daily journals and magazines available for reading. From there, the route leads up through a central void with diagonal staircases connecting seven alternating levels of books and resources. As one progresses, the welcoming and open atmosphere becomes more intimate and domestic. Sofas, chairs and small magazine racks located by windows on each level encourage readers to relax and spend time on the premises. They are a welcome relief in a building that tirelessly demands one's visual attention.

ADDRESS Het Baken/Stadhuisplein, Almelo
PROJECT ARCHITECT Henk Döll
GETTING THERE 4-minute walk from the Almelo station
ACCESS open

Overijssel

Mecanoo Architecten bv 1991–94

Mecanoo Architecten bv 1991–94

Rijksmuseum Twenthe, Enschede

When the Rijksmuseum Twenthe's director, Dr Dorothee Cannegieter, needed to refurbish the building, originally built in 1929, she consulted the *Rijksbouwmeester* for a suitable architect. Ben van Berkel was suggested after two other offices did not work out. Van Berkel renovated the old galleries and built a new wing for contemporary art and temporary exhibitions.

The floor plan is based on a pentangle with an inner courtyard. The first noticable intervention is a sculptural and dynamic rampway that signals a change in the old museum. The reception area remained unchanged except for the sculptural metal benches. From here the museum branches in two directions: to the right are galleries of work from the thirteenth to eighteenth centuries; to the left is the modern wing of nineteenth- and twentieth-century art.

A café in the central area adjacent to the courtyard, designed by Lodewijk Baljon, is the connection between the old and new sections of the museum. Here a strikingly dynamic expression – moulded concrete, angular features and specially designed furniture – shows the museum's willingness to embrace contemporary design. The new wing at the north-western corner of the triangle is open and light, and reverses the spectator's relationship to the art. Accessed via a small ramp, the viewer is put on stage in a room where the floor is raised 30 centimetres higher than the existing floor. The slanted ground and terraced ceiling establish an animated space that derives from the visitors' passing movement. The distressed stucco walls reflect a compromise between client and architect: van Berkel wanted untreated concrete while Cannegieter thought stucco was more suitable for showing art. Van Berkel cleverly integrated a ventilation system in a display that is simultaneously sculptural and functional.

The wing with twentieth-century art, a renovation of one arm of the

Overijssel

Van Berkel & Bos Architecten bv 1992–96

Overijssel

Van Berkel & Bos Architecten bv 1992–96

old building, is breathtaking in its lighting and spatial effects: Van Berkel heightened door frames and ceilings to create the feeling of endless space. A direct viewline throughout the wing means that visitors are never disorientated, something that was a problem in the older plan. The lighting, which alternates from vertical to horizontal in successive galleries, also creates a rhythmic pattern.

ADDRESS Lasondersingel 129–131, Enschede
PROJECT ARCHITECT Ben van Berkel
CLIENT Rijksgebouwendienst, Directie Oost, Arnhem
GETTING THERE 10-minute walk from Enschede station (follow signs)
ACCESS open; entrance fee

Overijssel

Van Berkel & Bos Architecten bv 1992–96

Van Berkel & Bos Architecten bv 1992–96

Gelderland

Housing and shops, Gerard Noodtstraat, Nijmegen 140
Print workshop, Ede 142
House of Fine Arts, Apeldoorn 144
Porter's Lodges, Park Hoge Veluwe 148
Isala College, Silvolde 150

Housing and shops, Gerard Noodtstraat, Nijmegen

In its attempt to achieve total mobility, Western culture is in a constant state of travel that affects even the most domestic environments. This nomadic spirit seems to have fuelled the design of this housing block, where the car park is not tucked away, but actually floats above the roof.

The area released by the rather unconventional roof allows for a communal garden behind the building and a strip of public green in front. The move cleverly blends the seven-storey structure, recessed slightly from the street, with the perimeter of the existing buildings. The dwellings are accessed by two sets of galleries that switch from front to back halfway down the block to diversify the appearance of the façade. At the same point the slab's axis is slightly rotated to break up the linearity of the design. A vertical accent, which loosens the block's horizontality, is given by the vehicle elevator, staircases and various programmes that stick through the layer of the galleries.

The wealth of material applied, ranging from corrugated steel, face concrete, timber, black brick, and steel grills, follows the logic that a housing block as vehicle carrier has to make a stately impression. The contrast between the cool, serialised concrete elements and the tactility of timber-clad volumes relies on the theatricality of their arrangement.

Although it seems that the design parameters were extended at every possible level, it is the unexpected inclusion of the car park that creates the building's charm. Yet the design remains a superficial exploration of the possibilities of the mobile and private spheres – a formal exercise.

ADDRESS Gerard Noodtstraat, Nijmegen
GETTING THERE walking distance from Nijmegen station
ACCESS none

De Architectengroep/Bjarne Mastbroek 1992–96

De Architectengroep/Bjarne Mastbroek 1992–96

Print workshop, Ede

Almost every Dutch architect and critic said that we must meet Willem Jan Neutelings. He is the designer of the moment, the architect's architect. His approach to architecture is typical of ex-OMA employees: an intense reading of the existing conditions that drives the design to regions yet unimagined. Like MVRDV, who take this philosophy to extreme lengths, Neutelings and his young colleague, Michiel Riedijk, test the accepted boundaries and notions of architecture. For this project, a new headquarters for Veenman printers, the aim was to articulate space for the two sections of the company: the offices and printing rooms with accompanying storage. The usual binarism of such quasi-industrial workshops, where workers and administrators inhabit separate parts of the building, has been done away with, the architects integrating the whole with a combined floorplan.

Located in a typical industrial neighbourhood, the building is sited around a courtyard garden designed by landscape impresarios West 8. Visitors enter through an aedicular entrance in the façade marked with a giant V. The use of lettering for load-bearing is reminiscent of the Minaertgebouw (see page 160). The most poetic part of the design, however, is the glazed area on the façade where a text by K Schippers is printed. It wraps around the building seven times. In all, the brilliant simplicity of the design is what makes Neutelings and Riedijk among the most popular of Dutch architects.

ADDRESS Maxwellstraat, Ede
DESIGN TEAM Willem Bruijn, Dirk van den Heuvel, Andy Woodcock
CONSULTANTS West 8 Landscape Architects, Rotterdam
CLIENT Veenman Printers, Wageningen
ACCESS none

Gelderland

Neutelings Riedijk Architecten bv 1995–96

Neutelings Riedijk Architecten bv 1995–96

House of Fine Arts, Apeldoorn

Apeldoorn is known for the Centraal Beheer, Herman Hertzberger's structuralist monument completed in 1972. Twenty years later, Rudy Uytenhaak, a member of the generation that followed structuralism while a student, has finished a cultural centre nearby. Although the buildings have completely different functions, they have a common denominator in the central design ideas of communication and visual connections. However, the House of Fine Arts is more restrained in its interpretations of these themes than the Centraal Beheer, which is open-ended.

Four institutions are integrated in the cultural centre: an art-lending library, a music school, De Gigant youth centre, and De Doekom art educational programme, which is aimed at adults. While the institutions function independently, they also profit from the concentration of cultural activities. Uytenhaak has had to come to grips with the different demands of each institution, such as their varied entrances and opening times, and has accommodated elegantly the resulting level of complexity. The centre's elongated body consists of two stacked, rectangular volumes that penetrate each other at an angle. A red brick wall runs through the whole length of the building at the plane of intersection, both separating and connecting individual parts and functions through its openings that close off and bring together. Entering from Nieuwmanstraat, a slope leads to the *souterrain*, which creates a generous foyer for the theatre and cinema auditoria of De Gigant. A small concert venue is also situated at the end of this concourse. The foyer, bounded by the masonry wall, works as a distribution hub crossed by various routes that link the art educational facilities with the music school and the café on the street front. There is a sense of a two-faced building: on one side De Gigant, whose introverted programmes shy from the outside and, on the other, the light-flooded interior terraces of the art-lending space.

Ir. Rudy Uytenhaak 1990–94

Gelderland

Gelderland

Ir. Rudy Uytenhaak 1990–94

This polarity is extended to the art centre's placement and the links it establishes with its surroundings. The curved entrance façade displays an urban motif that draws on the passing crowds of Nieuwmanstraat. On the rearside a stepped terrace fades into an open yard elaborating on the theme of a civic square as meeting place. Although the assumption that the building should be tied into its context by means of a shared public space is correct, the terrace-staircase combination does not lead anywhere but to a blank façade. More an architectural prop than the development of an internal logic, the rearside does not add up to much more than a pleasant place to sit in summer.

The House of Fine Arts walks a tightrope between success and failure, and there are moments of both. In several instances the programme does not reach its full potential. This could have been avoided as Uytenhaak displays his skill in the carefully balanced relationships within the building. Yet, by dividing the problems into smaller, more manageable, pieces, he misses the opportunity to derive a grand gesture, a problem accentuated by his concern for the integrity of the detailing.

ADDRESS Nieuwmanstraat, Apeldoorn
CLIENT Gemeente Apeldoorn
DESIGN TEAM Tiemen Koetsier, Jerôme Adema
GETTING THERE 5-minute walk from Apeldoorn station
ACCESS open

Ir. Rudy Uytenhaak 1990–94

Gelderland

Ir. Rudy Uytenhaak 1990–94

Porter's Lodges, Park Hoge Veluwe

On their 60th anniversary, De Hoge Veluwe national park invited designs for three porter's lodges. They needed a kiosk for ticket sales and the renting of bicycles for the Kroller-Mueller Museum in the park. MVRDV's scheme is based on three variations of a house with a saddle roof.

In each location the basic house type is morphed, creating shapes strangely reminiscent of Bruno Taut's crystalline architecture of the 1920s. The materials elaborate further the formal differentiations that are only restrained by the physical limits of Cor-ten steel, timber and masonry respectively. True to MVRDV's maxim of exaggerating the limits of design, each structure is conceived as a single surface to heighten its monolithic presence. The building's function is only apparent during opening hours when a surprisingly solid-looking brick, steel or timber wall metamorphoses to a shutter that reveals the awning of the ticket counter. The brick type posed considerable problems during construction, only solved when a compound was developed with the strength necessary for the roof details.

The consistent use of pure materials reveals that architectural riches can be found in paying attention to ordinary evidence. MVRDV is part of the generation that enjoys amplifying the utterly normal to such a degree that the commonplace becomes distinct.

ADDRESSES Houtkantweg 9, Otterlo (brick); Houtkantweg 13, Hoenderloo (steel); Koningenweg 13, Rijzenburg (timber)
DESIGN TEAM Winy Maas, Jacob van Rijs, Nathalie de Vries, Joost Glissener, E Didyk, A Mulder, J van Dijk
CLIENT Stichting Het Nationale Park De Hoge Veluwe
BUS 110 from Ede/Wageningen station or Apeldoorn station
ACCESS open

Gelderland

MVRDV 1994–97

Gelderland

MVRDV 1994–97

Isala College, Silvolde

When lecturing about the work of Mecanoo, Francine Houben illustrated her sources of inspiration. On her travels in North America and the Far East she encountered and documented textures, colours and materials that would resurface in later projects. Attaining more than a formal status the references also left their cultural imprint on some of the projects' central design ideas. The Isala College breathes the open atmosphere of an American university campus. Sited in lush green lawns, surrounded by a pastoral landscape, the secondary school is a telling demonstration that cerebral activities are best supported by a serene atmosphere. The functions of the college are in an ensemble of two distinct volumes. Notably the softly shaped gymnasium protruding half way from the elongated body of classrooms seems to borrow from Alvar Aalto's Nordic elegance. The deep brown of the vertically ordered wooden elements contrasts favourably with the communal lawn. Both backdrop and counterpiece, the wing of classrooms is orientated along an oaken-lined alleyway passing behind the school. The composition draws on the beauty and tranquillity of the setting and attempts to internalise it in a series of panoramic views. Parallel to these vistas, the inner spatial relations are relaxed by split levels and corridors, whose diminishing breadth break with their linearity. All would be in harmony but for a minor spoiling of the view of the green by the column grid of the opposite façade. Mecanoo suffers the fate of the *Musterschüler* (class pet), whose otherwise immaculate record is stained by such a small mishap.

ADDRESS Laan van Schuylenburch 8, Silvolde
CLIENT Katholieke Stichting voor Voortgezet Onderwijs, Oude IJssel
BUS 2 from Terborg station
ACCESS by appointment only

Gelderland

Mecanoo Architecten bv 1990–93

Mecanoo Architecten bv 1990–93

Utrecht

Two-family house, Utrecht 154

VSB Building, Utrecht 158

Minnaertgebouw, Utrecht 160

Educatorium, Utrecht 164

Faculty for Economics and Management, Utrecht 168

Rembrandthage apartments, Nieuwegein 170

Leidse Rijn urban development 172

Heat Transfer Station, Utrecht 176

50/10kv distributing substation, Amersfoort 178

Koekoeksweg housing, Amersfoort 180

Russian Palace, Amersfoort 182

Child daycare centre, Soest 184

Two-family house, Utrecht

Situated on a park in a posh residential district of Utrecht, this two-family house is a striking achievement in private domestic architecture. Just a short cycle ride from the Gerrit Rietveld's Schroeder House, the project neighbours three houses that are monuments to modernism and lives up to the reputation of its impressive predecessors.

The project began when two business people, who often travel for long periods, decided they wanted to build a *pied à terre* on the site. The amount of money needed to secure the site and the construction of a house proved out of the reach of their budget. Therefore, they pooled resources with another couple, both landscape architects, who knew Winy Maas from MVRDV. Unfortunately, the former couple had more money to invest and a 60/40 ratio proved challenging for a two-family house design. The uneven distribution created much friction between the parties! The landscape architects wanted MVRDV to design the house, while the business people were strongly against this. What made the situation even more complicated was the former couple's architect of choice, Bjarne Mastbroek, whose contributions somehow had to be integrated into the scheme.

The resolution to the problems came in a highly innovative spacial rearrangement of the interior of the house. Instead of a traditional vertical border between families or a division by storey, the boundary snakes through the volume giving generous expansions to each inhabitant on alternating levels. Using a situation in which each tenant is dependent on the other, MVRDV turned a dilemma into a strength by cleverly rearranging the spaces.

A height restriction on the street façade was circumvented by the architects who raised the ground level by a metre to achieve the height desired. The simple, box-like construction is broken up by two tones of green glass

MVRDV, Bjarne Mastbroek 1995–97

MVRDV, Bjarne Mastbroek 1995–97

panels that appear to be unevenly patterned along the brown plywood façade, which seems extremely vulnerable to the elements and was a result of budget restrictions. The use of two materials echoes the layout and spaces of interior of the house: communal areas are clad in glass while private spaces, such as bedrooms and bathrooms, are covered by solid material. The contrast in tones of glass cleverly serves further to emphasise the boundary between neighbours by subtly marking the space of each resident. A garden to the rear, however, reminds visitors that although the neighbours have clearly negotiated their interior territory, they must cooperate on use of the shared land.

ADDRESS Koningslaan, Utrecht
DESIGN TEAM Winy Maas, Jacob van Rijs, Nathalie de Vries, Mike Booth, Bjarne Mastbroek/De Architectengroep
CLIENTS Families Koek and Wesseling
BUS 3 to Mecklenburglaan
ACCESS none

Utrecht

MVRDV, Bjarne Mastbroek 1995–97

MVRDV, Bjarne Mastbroek 1995–97

VSB Building, Utrecht

Towering over the eastern section of Utrecht, the head office for VSB is a generic high-rise office building that offers few architectural surprises. A slim, white, 17-storey slab is anchored perpendicularly by two low-rise structures: a transparent, rectangular building to the west and a wedged-in, semicircular auditorium to the east. United by an arch-shaped vestibule, the ensemble makes an obvious reference to Le Corbusier's design for the Palace of the Soviets of 1931. How far the VSB office engages with the implicit social scope remains questionable.

The first indication of ultra-slick corporate attitude is found on the exterior: giant metal sculptures flank the building to the front and add the only bit of colour aside from the VSB logo at the top. A posse of security men serves to deter casual visitors. Once inside, a vast lobby filled with art provides a serene location. As one transfers to the levels above in the fully glazed external elevator, the tower's unimaginative floor1plans become evident. They are only broken by the fabulous double-storey spaces on the 15th and 16th floors that boast panoramic views of Utrecht but which are accessible only to members of the board and their guests. Common employees have to make do with a garden and a bridge on the site's northern edge that offers some reprieve from the indoor environment. One does not, however, get a feeling of comfort or welcome in the green area. Rather, the immaculate precision of West 8's landscape design aligns itself with the corporate alienation of the built structure.

ADDRESS Archimedeslaan, Utrecht
PROJECT ARCHITECTS Peter Vermeulen, Roeland Driessen
CONSULTANTS West 8 Landscape Architects, Rotterdam
BUS 11, 30, 31, 42, 51, 96–99 to Pythagoraslaan
ACCESS garden only

Utrecht

Van Mourk Vermeulen Architecten bv 1991–2

Van Mourk Vermeulen Architecten bv 1991–2

Minnaertgebouw, Utrecht

In 1986 the Office for Metropolitan Architecture (OMA) drafted the masterplan for the expansion of the Uithof, the campus of the University of Utrecht. The plan eventually was carried out by a former OMA employee, Aart Zaijer. Tapping into the potential of the immense spaces between buildings, the policy tries to establish a new relationship to the ground, something conspicuously ignored by the existing educational infrastructure of the 1970s.

The Minnaertgebouw, named after a famous geophysicist, holds a key corner plot in the 'north western cluster'. Serving the Faculties of Mathematics, Information Technology and Geophysics, it is connected to the neighbouring buildings by footbridges, which lead directly to a central hall that is the manifestation of a formidable interpretation of the brief. A roof that is intended to leak, entire sections that are unheated and an outer shell analogous to reptile skin speak of an edifice reluctantly fulfilling common architectural pretensions.

The brief defined precise gross and net floor areas; these translate into service elements such as circulation or emergency routes, and the original functions of classrooms, laboratories and a restaurant. The major difference though was that the former did not underlie the stringent Dutch climate requirements. Neutelings Riedijk architects tested the consequences of streamlining the efficiency of the plan layout and the resulting availability of unregulated, yet budgeted, floor area. The difference between gross and net space added to a vast interior that was neither defined in terms of climatic control nor outlined in the brief. This 'absence' acquires the role of a gathering hall and central hub which distributes students to seminar rooms and the canteen.

When it is raining, openings in the ceiling of the *aula* let water gush down to an interior pond. From there it is pumped through a series of

Neutelings Riedijk Architecten bv 1994–97

Neutelings Riedijk Architecten bv 1994–97

ceiling grills in the lower floor – air conditioning for the computer laboratories. Afterwards the warmed rainwater flows back to the pond, where it cools during the night ready for a new cycle the next day. A slope in the floor of the assembly room leads unceremoniously into the pond without any indication of its edge. Wet seasons are registered by the rising water level that subsequently reduces the dry area of the hall. In winter the pond is supposed to freeze over. A refuge from the biting chill is offered by a row of heated cubicles like train compartments.

The outer appearance is a token of Neutlings Riedijk's current interest in connective materials that defy separate notions of ceiling, wall and floor. In reality, however, the red-pigmented, sprayed-on concrete façade is far less exciting than earlier computer renderings where the building's rippled texture resembled the skin of a lizard. The amount of concrete that could be applied each day handicapped the idea of continuity, and the disruptive junctions between *giornate* made the exterior strangely reminiscent of scar tissue. This ugliness and the refusal of the projection of an artistic ideal is certainly part of Neutelings' past at OMA. The Minnaertgebouw might be grotesque and at times imperfect, but the architects extracted the imminent collectivity of a seemingly uncontroversial proposition.

ADDRESS Leuvenlaan, De Uithof, Utrecht
DESIGN TEAM Willem Jan Neutelings, Michiel Riedijk, Jonathan Woodroffe, Evert Crols, Burton Hamfeldt, Chidi Onwuka
CLIENT Universiteit Utrecht
BUDGET NFL22 million
BUS 12, 12S, 280S–284S
ACCESS open

Neutelings Riedijk Architecten bv 1994–97

Educatorium, Utrecht

The Educatorium, OMA's first university building, continues to investigate numerous themes outlined in their earlier work. Ludwig Mies van der Rohe's conception of an open plan is injected with a well-measured dose of dirty realism. The work of this office, which prides itself on having no style, can be categorised roughly as: the compact urbanism, such as the Grand Palais, Lille, and structures that employ morphed or continuous surfaces, as found in the Kunsthal, Rotterdam (see page 256). The Educatorium on the campus of the University of Utrecht is firmly of the latter type. By means of angled, interlocked and seamless ground planes, different uses and meanings are forced together in a hard-edged montage.

On entering the foyer, a ramp bifurcates to lead down to the canteen and up to the two auditoria on the first floor. Behind the projection booths the slant wraps up to be assimilated by the ceiling, which in turn becomes the floor slab of the examination spaces above. To a certain extent these formal stunts are merely design rhetorics as the overall quality stems from the shrewd appropriation of precedents in architectural history and contemporary art. The design achieves some of its most hilarious moments from a variety of *trompe l'œils* that sabotage stable notions of inside/outside and open/closed. A glass section of a balcony on the first floor has a view of the students queuing in the canteen below. Large window panels allow daylight to penetrate deeply into the building. Although OMA's attitude sneers at such petty concerns, the reflective surfaces seem to expand the space infinitely, clearly evoking the aesthetic sensibility of the American artist Dan Graham. The sheer number and eclecticism of references condense a style which – while deriving from specific sources – has to be regarded as autonomous and personal to Rem Koolhaas.

Lecture halls and offices are separate from the external skin in an open-

Utrecht

Office for Metropolitan Architecture 1992–97

plan arrangement that is extended to the third dimension. Freed from each other, planes and masses stage a spatial tension which is very skilfully balanced. The drama of the promenade warps the visitor through the building without taking a passage twice. This impression is reinforced by the unfinished and mercilessly jammed-together materials that indulge in an almost baroque splendour. Rather than being smoothed under the compulsive gloss of 'good detailing', the contradictions of the construction techniques are made visible.

Being more than an even distribution on a concrete slab the programmes also have vertical repercussions on structure and organisation. The Vierendeel beam that stiffens the perimeter of the auditorium level liberates the restaurant below from being engulfed by a forest of concrete columns. Koolhaas champions such structural hybridity to support his theory that architecture is not legitimised by a linear order and composition, but by the intelligent and precise use of its instruments. In doing so he unearths a hidden dimension that articulates freedoms, which are indeed poetic and beautiful.

ADDRESS Leuvenlaan, De Uithof, Utrecht
DESIGN TEAM Rem Koolhaas, Christophe Cornubert, Gary Bates, Richard Eelman
CONSULTANTS Adviesburo voor Bouwtechniek, Ingenieursburo Linssen
CLIENT Universiteit Utrecht
FLOOR AREA 10,000 square metres
BUDGET NFL29 million
BUS 12, 12S, 280S–284S
ACCESS open

Office for Metropolitan Architecture 1992–97

Office for Metropolitan Architecture 1992–97

Faculty for Economics and Management, Utrecht

Mecanoo's efficient and no-nonsense contribution to the university campus, the Faculty for Economics and Management, leaves the viewer intrigued about its aims. Although a marvellous design, the architecture does not take a stand and lacks an inner attitude. The entrance, a glass frontage along Padualaan, commands a view of the communal areas and the lecture theatres. Located in four volumes protruding from the translucent enclosure, the auditoria are the most distinct features.

While walking around inside, the route circles three themed patios. Of these only the jungle-like bamboo grove is accessible, the Japanese and the water gardens are for visual pleasure only. Obviously the latter's tranquil atmosphere supports the focus on the studies, yet it does not go beyond aesthetics and consider anything else. There is a discrepancy between the visual richness of the steel grid and timber-clad courtyard walls, and the lack of activities they stimulate. Profane elements such as service pipes and neon lights are subjected to the same treatment as far more significant parts of the architecture. The design is so thoroughly conceived, its desire to beautify every part so overwhelming, that it becomes compulsive. Mecanoo is a highly competent architectural firm that has not lost faith in the profession's aptitude for conciliation. Their wish to exercise such a level of aesthetic control sits uncomfortably between the quest for a better architectural environment and the paradox of a contradicting urban cultural condition.

ADDRESS Padualaan, De Uithof, Utrecht
CLIENT Stichting FEHU, Utrecht
BUS 12, 12S, 280S–284S
ACCESS open

Mecanoo Architecten bv 1991–95

Mecanoo Architecten bv 1991–95

Rembrandthage apartments, Nieuwegein

The expanding conurbations with their of lack of urban references are a difficult challenge for an architect. To the south of Utrecht, however, Kees Christiaanse Architecten has designed four apartment blocks for the subsidised housing sector that defy the setting's dullness and small budget.

In a refinement of their earlier work, the office has moved on from reductive excavations (see page 306) towards a stricter analytical method. Kees Christiaanse argues that the use of architecture is to 'investigate how far design should execute control and at what moment it should stop executing control'. The formal simplicity of the Nieuwegein project is misleading as the sober exterior cloaks its internal qualities. Each block is segmented in halves that are rotated against each other, exposing the apartments to maximum sunlight. One volume sits elevated on a plinth of storage spaces which twists the building's roof line. Wedged between the two masses is a fully glazed, light-filled atrium giving the flats a second orientation. As Christiaanse explains, the 'secret agenda was to articulate a collective space between the private sphere and the public realm; spaces that can be colonised'.

The six-storey atrium is intersected by steel footbridges whose original function is to shorten escape routes to the distances demanded by fire regulations. The views to the exterior public space and the invigoration of the interior indicate that the wealth of this project lies in a compact collectivity.

ADDRESS Rembrandthage, Galecop, Nieuwegein
DESIGN TEAM Kees Christiaanse, Ruurd Roorda, Kees Slotboom
TRAM 1 BUS 292, 320 to Betauweg
ACCESS none

Utrecht

Kees Christiaanse Architects and Planners 1993–95

Utrecht

Kees Christiaanse Architects and Planners 1993–95

Leidse Rijn urban development

Dutch cityscapes are currently undergoing the most profound changes since the post-war period. A governmental programme, VINEX, outlines an estimated need for 800,000 new dwellings by 2005. One VINEX location is Leidse Rijn, west of Utrecht, where over the next 20 years 30,000 dwellings will be constructed. The time and scale of the given task makes a plan based on a premeditated form and organisation of this future city futile by default. Arbitrary changes to lifestyles and a transient culture prove too complex to be predictable and adequately addressed by such a method. Urban administrator Riek Bakker selected the young practice Max. Architecture and Urbanism as part of an interdisciplinary team to develop the urban plan. The commission equates such young practices with an openness and capacity to solve such planning problems.

Rients Dijkstra concedes that it 'was most astonishing that the city actually decided to go through with it'. Working in collaboration with the architectural theoreticians Crimson, Max. created six indices for a flexible strategy that could accommodate the shifting variables driving urbanisation. They employed individual criteria such as spreading, persons per area, programmatic mixing, spatial boundaries and level of architectural control as decision-making tools. The future Leidse Rijn crystallises from clearly defined trajectories that – without compromising the basic principles of the plan – constantly reconfigure according to shifting economical, political and environmental issues. In place of an ideology that provides guarantees of stability, form and coherence, this brand of urbanism claims the capacity to create a field of opportunities. Rients Dijkstra elaborates: 'I rather try to find what other things emerge from the way people lead their lives nowadays. If I say emerge, I put myself in a role of an arranger and not a dictator. I think the best thing we can do is to provide situations which are very fertile to contemporary activ-

Max. Architectuur Stedenbouw 1995–96

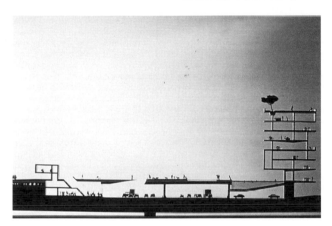

Max. Architectuur Stedenbouw 1995–96

ities, so that they can happen instead of trying to control a specific nostalgic type'. Although Max. considers a growing web of traffic infrastructure to be the pacemaker of the development, the design avoids creating a watershed condition caused by major routes. Within 300 metres of the A2 motorway, the causal relationship between heavy traffic and noise regulations forbids the construction of housing. This buffer would not only cut off Leidse Rijn from Utrecht, but also would tie large amounts of green space along the routes. By displacing and submerging a 2-km-long strip of motorway, the 'saved' green area becomes a huge central park. Simultaneously, the tunnel restores a continuous morphology between Utrecht and the new city. Above the road, housing meets infrastructure, offices and leisure areas, a combination that does not occur in orthodox town planning. To convince local and federal authorities to pay the additional cost of the tunnel, research was conducted into the effects of the shorter, covered motorway: results showed a significant reduction of polluting emissions, a fact that even the governmental bodies could not ignore. What made it all gel? Rients Dijkstra's answer reads like a mission statement: 'You can guess or synthesise a problem and a solution and then one in twenty times come up with a good scheme or you can do a serious investigation to find out what the stakes are and do it well ten to twenty times. I completely disagree that research is less interesting than fantasy … it is the other way around'.

ADDRESS Leidse Rijn, west of central Utrecht
DESIGN TEAM Rients Dijkstra, Kirsten van der Berg, Arjan Klok, Catherine Visser, Arno de Vries
CLIENT Gemeente Utrecht
ACCESS open

Utrecht

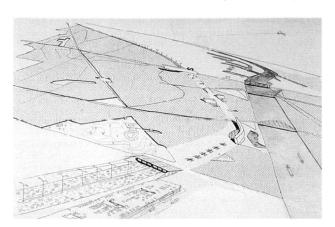

Max. Architectuur Stedenbouw 1995–96

Heat Transfer Station, Utrecht

The WOS (Warmte Overdracht Station), a forerunner of the urbanisation of the Leidse Rijn, is a mediation between technology, environmental concerns and symbolism for a city that has not yet arrived. The station extracts surplus energy from the cooling water of a nearby district heating plant and the thermal efficiency of the recycling process is sufficient to heat about 11,000 homes.

Because the brief did not have a programme to work with, NL Architects invented uses for a box in an urbane area. Their presentation folder shows a latex-clad S&M dominatrix to illustrate the imperviousness of a new rubber compound used for the building's outer skin. This skin-deep reference indicates the superficiality of both the iconography, which wields an explicit sexual reference as a metaphor for a profane utilitarian building, and the general cultural weight that the architects assign to it.

Expressions of the individual desires and expectations of urban life are acknowledged in the unfolded elevation of the building. Many activities are found interwoven in the continuous band of the façade: spy holes to the interior; breeding niches for birds; an artificial climbing wall with a basketball hoop. The building's diverse functions make it a commodity that can be appropriated for different means. The WOS materialises fleeting qualities such as the ordinary and banal while celebrating the present absence of meaning. Yet, it has still to demonstrate that the reliance on the loose network of (ab)use will influence its environment.

ADDRESS Rijksstraatweg, Utrecht
DESIGN TEAM P Brannenberg, W van Dijk, K Klaasse, M Linnemann
CLIENT Gemeente Utrecht
BUS 127, 128, 180, 245, 428 to Park Rheyngaerde
ACCESS perimeter only

Utrecht

NL Architects 1997–98

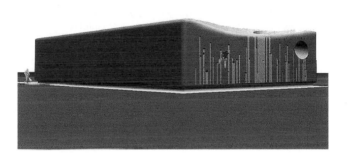

NL Architects 1997–98

50/10kv distributing substation, Amersfoort

Ben van Berkel and Caroline Bos' power station is an example of their dynamic yet careful approach to design. The project is one of several in Amersfoort (their Karbouw headoffice on Basicweg is also worth a visit) where the architects' were given their first crack at building.

The substation is in essence a two-part shell covering three electrical transformers. The architects have highlighted the division between the two volumes by using contrasting materials: conductive aluminium is set against insulating basalt lava in all-over façades broken only by a small, timber-clad entrance. The disparity in volumes is further accentuated by vertical and horizontal shifts. In their trademark style, van Berkel and Bos have made nothing straight: instead slight angles give the building a dynamic feel. The lack of a need for light allows the structure to be window-free, giving the exterior a slick, neo-minimal look.

The brilliance of the design lies in its simplicity and sculptural quality. Because it is visible from many directions, including from the feeder road and passing trains, the station's aesthetic impact certainly would have been a driving force in the design.

ADDRESS Smallepad 2, Amersfoort
PROJECT ARCHITECT Ben van Berkel
GETTING THERE 2-minute walk from Amersfoort station
ACCESS none

Utrecht

Van Berkel & Bos Architecten bv 1989–93

Utrecht

Van Berkel & Bos Architecten bv 1989–93

Koekoeksweg housing, Amersfoort

The stringent use of floor area is a permanent constraint when designing social housing, and often an architect's inventiveness is inhibited by the conservatism and small budgets of the housing corporations. Kees Christiaanse's project in the east of Amersfoort displays one way of relieving the corset of predetermined spaces. Balconies are slotted between the external access gallery and the building, effectively becoming a buffer zone of small terraces. Their breadth is continued inside by the unusually wide hallways that double as living rooms. Made entirely of timber, the projecting structure serves as a kind of communal meeting place. This sensitive threshold between the private and public domains demonstrates what seems to be a major concern of Christiaanse's practice:

FM Was it actually a request from the client to have the timber?
Kees Christiaanse No not at all. They hated it.
KB Was it too expensive?
KC No it wasn't expensive, but they are afraid of the cost of maintenance and of the look, when it becomes grey and weathered. We like it, but the inhabitants don't. It is always a fight. On the other side, they also see it is a warm material, so they have an ambivalent attitude towards the use of timber. We were able to prove that the gallery system was actually cheaper than a concrete structure. That made it clear that we could do it. This was very special, there are not so many housing corporations that would let me do this. I think we were very lucky, because some of the corporations would have told us to use brick or go away.

ADDRESS Koekoeksstraat, Spreeuwenstraat, Amersfoort
BUS 5, 6 to Lageweg
ACCESS none

Utrecht

Kees Christiaanse Architects and Planners 1995–97

Kees Christiaanse Architects and Planners 1995–97

Russian Palace, Amersfoort

Zielhorst, a northern subdivision of Amersfoort, diverges from a typical peripheral neighbourhood. In a programme tastefully called 'de etalage' (showcase) residents could pick the architect of their future homestead from a shortlist of well-known names. Wiel Arets, van Berkel & Bos, Ton Alberts and Max van Huut were among the practices invited to participate. The plan went as far as associating the residents' addresses with architectural history: street names refer to the giants of twentieth-century modernism. Democratic pretensions hidden under the cloak of architectural diversity act as commercially motivated vehicles.

Piet Blom realised that such an overabundance of individual choice would drown any architectural distinction and as such his Russian Palace opts for a memorable alternative. Ignoring the respectability of the given task, the project unites Blom's aversion to this design feast with the unsurprisingly bad taste of his client. The onion-shaped domes on top of what appears to be a standard suburban dwelling bear more resemblance to a theme park attraction than to the Siberian timber architecture they are loosely modelled on. Yet this architectural one-liner plays no part in any urban synthesis as it simply affirms the coexistence of individual projects one perceives as equivalent and unconnected.

A model district like Zielhorst creates a paradox for the profession by the conformist ideal it imposes. What is even more disturbing is that its narcissism suggests that individuality can only be achieved in a culture of consensus.

ADDRESS Haussmanstraat/Molierestraat, Amersfoort
CLIENT Herman de Val
BUS 12, 96, 103 to Spothall Zielhorst, then a 5-minute walk
ACCESS none

Piet Blom 1991–93

Piet Blom 1991–93

Child daycare centre, Soest

This child daycare centre differs in appearance and function from any other kindergarten. Rather than focusing on the children in a saccharine-sweet patronising manner, the project envisages a kind of anti-establishment institution. The children are given a freedom usually denied in an environment that supposedly teaches them to be functioning citizens. It is not about regulating but about deregulating, creating zones where the children can be themselves, hidden away from the grown-up world in a three-dimensional playground.

The kindergarten is in a refurbished school. The two wings house the play hall and the nursery area; a small addition contains all the administrative functions. Because of pressure from the all-powerful Welstands-commissie – a committee that advises on the issuing of building permits on aesthetic grounds – it was decided to leave the exterior unchanged, but most of the internal space was released for the building's new function.

Two models are played out against each other: the protective world of a traditional daycare centre and the open-ended, anarchic approach which prioritises the children as social beings and future inhabitants. In a series of twisted, intersecting volumes, the intervention undermines any *a priori* understanding of programmatic content. Although the shapes of the play furniture are refreshingly diverse, their formal status enjoys less significance than the conceptual rigour of the scheme.

Whole sections of the building are allocated solely to the children. This domain, a maze of timber beams, plywood panels and steel-mesh, winds and turns above the open spaces of the ground floor. A dense fabric of boxes, bridges and niches stretches to the roof and becomes, to some extent, inaccessible even to an adult. Here the role of the supervisor and the supervised is reversed as it is the children who, hidden from view, can

DJ&V Architecten 1991–92

DJ&V Architecten 1991–92

spy from their elevated peepholes to the goings-on below.

On the ground floor the space has been left open for 'wheeled' activities with tricycles or scooters. Indeed, the floor is painted with road signs usually associated with motorways, while the main element, a disused Renault, is happily conquered by the children.

The project is not only unique in its inherent criticism of a traditional Kindergarten but also how the design team was set up. Originally the commission was acquired and the brief articulated by Mathijs Bouw, but instead of starting a practice on the strength of such a commission, he, Ton Venhoeven, Mirjam Galje, Daan Bakker and Kirsten van den Berg opted to collaborate as a committee for this project only. Accordingly, the decision avoided allocating authorship of a specific part, which would, as the architects felt, undermine the equality of a broad range of ideas and occurrences that are manifest in the end result. The rawness of the finish radiates an air of *ad hoc* decision-making that gives hints of the working process for both design and construction. This formidable project demonstrates in more than one way that architecture as a discipline can still offer a cultural perspective with social relevance.

ADDRESS Talmalaan 42, Soest
CLIENT Stichting Kindercentra, Soest
BUDGET NFL550,000
FLOOR AREA 710 square metres
GETTING THERE 5-minute walk from Soest/Dijk station
ACCESS only by appointment

Utrecht

DJ&V Architecten 1991–92

Utrecht

DJ&V Architecten 1991–92

Noord Brabant and Zeeland

Artoteek, Breda 190
Chassé Theatre, Breda 192
Fire station, Breda 196
De Pont Foundation, Tilburg 198
Tivoli parking garage, Tilburg 200
Neeltje Jans Water Pavilion, Oosterschelde 202

Artoteek, Breda

For a small town such as Breda there is a surprising emphasis on the arts. Herman Hertzberger's Chassé Theatre (see page 192) and his earlier arts media centre reflect a commitment to culture that seems unrivalled in similar Dutch towns. The artoteek exhibits the same spirit. This small project is more notable for its programme than for any architectural accomplishments. An artoteek is an art-lending library where original works of art – painting, sculpture, ceramics – can be hired on a monthly basis with an option to buy. With today's saturated art market, this is a clever resource for both artist and patron.

Hans von Heeswick designed a façade entirely of glass: it is clear on the ground floor to attract customers and opaque on the first and second floors to filter light and protect the works. Once inside, the exhibition spaces on all floors are linked via a quasi-industrial staircase. Offices, an art depot and storage space are on the top floor. The atmosphere throughout is one of chic simplicity. In all it is an impressive project on a restricted budget, the most interesting thing being the programme.

Noord Brabant and Zeeland

ADDRESS Boschstraat 22, Breda
GETTING THERE 5-minute walk from Breda station
ACCESS open

Hans von Heeswick 1989

Hans von Heeswick 1989

Chassé Theatre, Breda

The undulating roof of the Chassé Theatre boasts a prominent position in the otherwise non-eccentric skyline of Breda. Camouflaging the towering heights of two auditoria, the waves are decorative, but also play a functional role in the complicated design of the building. In this project Herman Hertzberger, one of the oldest generation of architects working in The Netherlands, breaks with his past role as 'the prophet of Structuralism' and takes on a more Rem Koolhaas-like approach to spatial play, relying on innovative organisational concepts rather than costly materials.

The city council gave a restrictive brief: three auditoria, two cinemas, offices, foyers, shops and bars to accommodate about 3000 arty folk and media people in a relatively small floor area. The site was equally problematic, situated between the old army barracks, the Kloosterkazerne, and new offices just outside the historic centre.

Hertzberger's solution uses the restrictions as organisational tools. Two stage towers are placed around a central backstage space. The resulting cumbersome volumes protrude in the public space, creating a promenade effect in the oddly shaped area inside, which contains several bars and seating areas. The area's colourful decor is enhanced by 29 structural columns, 28 of which are painted in varying colours. The use of such vibrant colour marks a renaissance in Hertzberger's typically sober approach to pigments, and the one column left as untreated concrete is a reminder of Hertzberger's less flamboyant past.

The theatres are designed for three separate uses: two black boxes seat 250 and 729 people respectively, the latter capable of holding 1250 standing for concerts or events. The highlight of the building is the largest and most histrionic auditorium of 1289 seats designed for operas and musicals. The fabulous space is punctuated by eight asymmetrically

Architectuurstudio Herman Hertzberger 1992–95

Architectuurstudio Herman Hertzberger 1992–95

suspended balconies that give superb views to the stage. The varying colours of the seats also show an unforeseen sense of play in the architect's work.

While the Chassé Theatre will undoubtedly attract visitors and recognition to this small town, it is also a successful project for the architect, proving that the unexpected is still possible from the most reliable of Dutch social architects.

Noord Brabant and Zeeland

ADDRESS Claudius Prinsenlaan 8, Breda
PROJECT ARCHITECT Willem van Winsen
CLIENT Gemeente Breda
GETTING THERE 5-minute walk from Breda station
ACCESS open

Architectuurstudio Herman Hertzberger 1992–95

Architectuurstudio Herman Hertzberger 1992–95

Fire station, Breda

The essence of this building can be summed up in how quickly you can leave it. Breda's new fire station is not determined by a stylistic idiom, but is to a significant extent the result of all-pervading efficient organisation. Dutch fire regulations require the brigade to be out of the building within 1 minute from the alarm going off and on site within another 6 minutes. Time is also a major factor for the life inside, where on-duty firefighters spend most of their week. Between emergency calls and exercises, the staff relax in their living quarters. An intimate atmosphere is the abiding trait of the communal rooms and the adjacent dormitories, which are embedded in series of three roof gardens. Yet Breda's Brandweer thrives on the combination of the overlapping educational, administrative and training functions that ensue in a sometimes surreal montage.

Michiel Riedijk I know everything about fire brigades by now. For example, they get into their dress while walking, get on the pole and then on to the truck. That takes approximately 50 seconds.
KB And there is a opening in the floor of the dormitory?
MR There is a main hall below that all the sleeping rooms connect to. The living room is hanging in the main hall and also the circulation of the offices passes through it, while firemen drop down on the poles, they kind of fall through the office level.
FM It is like a Monty Python sketch, where the executives are dropping by an office window, committing suicide because they are fired.
MR It has the same quality.

ADDRESS Tramsingel, Breda
GETTING THERE 5-minute walk from Breda station
ACCESS none

Noord Brabant and Zeeland

Neutelings Riedijk Architecten bv 1996–98

Neutelings Riedijk Architecten bv 1996–98

De Pont Foundation, Tilburg

The current trend for converting industrial spaces into galleries showing contemporary art includes certain internationally acclaimed examples such as the Saatchi Gallery and the forthcoming Tate Gallery at Bankside by Herzog and de Meuron, both in London. Although Tilburg is not normally considered a capital of culture, Benthem Crouwel's building for the Tilburg Foundation's collection of contemporary art is in the category of international highlights. By giving a well-conceived makeover to an old wool factory, the architects have created a strikingly beautiful museum.

The most important issue was the retention of the character of the original building, not only because it was useful but also to preserve the essence of the past. The roof and floor of the large hall were renovated and the walls restored. Any additions made to the original building, such as the entrance, toilet area, kitchen and bookshop, are accentuated to reinforce the integrity of the old building. The captivating quality of light is made possible through skylights that have a system of double glass filled with a white synthetic fibre. Light is filtered evenly throughout the main space, but aberrations in weather are noticeable inside. Each gallery has its own character deriving from their different finishes.

ADDRESS Wilhelminapark 1, Tilburg
DESIGN TEAM H Löhmann, A Staalenhoef
CLIENT De Pont Stichting
GETTING THERE 5-minute walk from Tilburg station or BUS 43 to Wilhelminaplein
ACCESS open; entrance fee

Noord Brabant and Zeeland

Benthem Crouwel Architecten bv 1990–92

Benthem Crouwel Architecten bv 1990–92

Tivoli parking garage, Tilburg

Multi-storey carparks are one type among modernity's bland hardware that, although omnipresent in city centres and latently interesting, are apparently unable to arouse the imagination of architects. The average parking garage is basically a stack of concrete slabs connected by a ramp. A regime of arbitrary criteria such as the height of a car antenna and lights bright enough only to reveal car keys mercilessly rules these spaces. It is only recently that these conditions, potentially unsafe for women on their own, forced the designers to put the car owner into the equation. Within this context, Benthem Crouwel, better known for their gleaming terminal at Schiphol airport (see page 64), built a carpark in Tilburg that is considered one of their finest projects.

In a bold move, the design merges ramps and parking decks, thus freeing itself from dull spatial constraints. A one-way system of alternating descending and ascending ramps creates a pervading effect of spatial diversity. The centrally located ramps also establish a surprising architectural promenade from the elevator to the vehicles. On top an open-air deck offers a view of Tilburg's roofscape. Back at street level, the façade of meshed steel panels contributes to the building's compact look. The overall translucent character, which has become a hallmark of the architect's work, is further enhanced by a strip of circular glass blocks in the floor that allow daylight to filter to lower levels. At night the blocks emit a blue light that gives an outlandish atmosphere to this sober and meritorious building.

ADDRESS Veemarkt, Tilburg
BUS 43–45 to Heuvel
GETTING THERE 5-minute from Tilburg station
ACCESS open

Noord Brabant and Zeeland

Benthem Crouwel Architecten bv 1992–95

Benthem Crouwel Architecten bv 1992–95

Neeltje Jans Water Pavilion, Oosterschelde

If architecture ever deserved to be discussed in the scientific terms of fluid and dynamic systems, such is the case for the recently opened Water Pavilion on Neeltje Jans island in the Oosterschelde. The theme of the building is centred around the cycles of fresh- and saltwater. Lars Spruybroek (NOX Architects) and Kas Oosterhuis (Oosterhuis Associates), both veterans of computer culture and architecture, have realised what critic Bart Lootsma described as 'the strangest commission one can think of'. Merging structure and exhibition content, the pavilion effortlessly leaps from the potential of liquid architecture to its realisation. As a consequence, the terminology inherent to the discipline falls short when describing a massive media-tectural apparatus that fuses architecture and electronic technology. The body of this 'machine' has two parts: Spruybroek's freshwater, or H2O, pavilion, followed by Oosterhuis' saltwater section. Both designs represent vastly different approaches to the brief. While NOX's silver-clad, morphed volume has a beautiful abstract quality; Oosterhuis' solution faintly resembles a whale and is an interpretation of the theme.

Spruybroek portrays his 60-metre-long succession of ellipses, whose scales and orientations alter as a 'metamorphosis of a doorstep' or a 'complicated corridor'. The form of this tube derives from samples taken of site conditions, which included gales and the groundwater level, that were subsequently translated to a bundle of spline curves.

The streamlined H2O pavilion is entered through a snout-like opening that leads into an ice-covered vestibule. The melted ice drips over the ground, forms a small stream and flows into the dark interior. The building is meant to be wet inside, and in the midst of water in all its manifestations, a media bombardment of slide projections, video beamers and

NOX Architecten and Oosterhuis Associates 1994–97

NOX Architecten and Oosterhuis Associates 1994–97

stroboscope flashes ensues. The message raises the awareness of the use and waste of fresh water. At the same time, the wet element steams, gurgles and is propelled from a variety of nozzles embedded in the surface that wraps around like a skin. Accompanied by a cacophony of artificial and splashing noises from hidden loudspeakers, this Dantesque inferno gives the impression of a theme park illusion. However, the interactive nature of the environment quickly becomes apparent: while walking through a projected grid, infrared sensors detect the movement and the projection is rippled by a wave, which rolls along with one's strides.

On a different topological level, the number of visitors and their level of activity changes the frequency of the pulsating illumination. And the installation is not restricted to a single person per sensor either. A group of nodes sticking from the wall/floor surface allows up to four visitors simultaneously to steer a projected computer graphic. The distorted graph renders the building's warped surfaces as a fleeting definition of the visitors' engagement with the structure. In that sense the architecture can be read as an extension of their bodies, as a prosthesis, which increases their sensorium and sphere of action. The ingenuity of NOX's design overlaps all these stimuli in a multilayered field of interaction, which sets forth unpredictable consequences and repercussions.

After the magnificent freshwater pavilion, the saltwater section by Oosterhuis is bound to be a disappointment. Where the former looked fluid in its seamless activation of space, the latter contains a multimedia presentation whose passive consumption compares unfavourably. The external climate factors that drive the video projections are never clear to the visitor. The most fundamental difference is the distinction of installation and architecture, a duality which is effectively blurred by Spruybroek's intervention.

NOX Architecten and Oosterhuis Associates 1994–97

Noord Brabant and Zeeland

NOX Architecten and Oosterhuis Associates 1994–97

Stepping out of the dark container, one has to acknowledge that two entirely different attitudes are at work. On one hand is Oosterhuis' understanding of the computer as a tool of production, which limits his structure to an anachronistic lesson in popular science. On the other hand is Spruybroek's integrative model that attempts boldly to go beyond the limitations of an architecture defined by a subject/object relationship. The result is an unsettling hybrid of a building that can be likened to a scientist's laboratory, where the seductive fruits of technology beckon. Although the underlying desire for an architecture that serves as a prosthesis remains partially unfulfilled, NOX's H2O pavilion is at present the most radical manifestation of the boundary between architecture and the digital domain.

Noord Brabant and Zeeland

ADDRESS Waterpark Neeltje Jans, Oosterschelde
DESIGN TEAM Lars Spruybroek, M Nio, J Almekinders, P Heymans, W Verbeek
CLIENT Ministry for Transport, Public Works and Water Management and Delta Expo
CAR N57 along Delta Works
BUS 104 from Hof van Tange bus stop, a 5-minute walk from Middelburg station
ACCESS open; entrance fee

NOX Architecten and Oosterhuis Associates 1994–97

NOX Architecten and Oosterhuis Associates 1994–97

Limburg

Academy of Fine Arts, Maastricht 210
AZL office, Heerlen 224
Bonnefantenmuseum, Maastricht 214
Police station, Vaals 220
Prinsenhoek Housing, Sittard 230
De Spiegel primary school, Maastricht 218

Academy of Fine Arts, Maastricht

The Academy of Fine Arts is one of Wiel Arets' earlier, more austere buildings. It sounds pretentious to departmentalise a body of work produced in little more than a decade into distinct projects, but there are entirely different results from the interpretation of corresponding programmes and briefs. The coarse whiteness and extensive use of large, translucent surfaces are little more than a foretaste of similar concerns that influenced the more sophisticated designs of the AZL office, Heerlen and Police Station, Vaals (both finished in 1995; see pages 224 and 220). The Academy, a project that earned Arets a nomination for the prestigious Mies van der Rohe award in 1994, has two introverted blocks straddling Herdenkingsplein. Constructed from a concrete skeleton with an infill of diaphanous glass bricks, the exterior is both mysterious and pristine. The main entrance, opposite the volume holding studios and workshops, leads into the reception area, from where ramps lead to the lecture theatre in the basement and the cafeteria above. The ramps are removed from the wall to allow daylight to penetrate the interior. As one descends, the diminishing illumination from above acts as a point of reference, reminding one of the point of departure and acting as an unsettling perception of time and distance. The use of light is discussed by Arets:

FM It is a nice metaphor, cinema and light. I think daylight has a very important role in the way you design.

Wiel Arets In cinema you sit in darkness and light enters the dark room and usually we don't think about that in architecture, you always think about the reverse. You think about the building and the sun and then sun giving light to the material. And I am quite interested in the reverse as well. When we design a building, I never want a building that is lit. And I think when you make a building you have to construct it in a

Wiel Arets & Associates 1989–93

Wiel Arets & Associates 1989–93

way that either by night light is doing something to it or during the day, changing the interior.

The Academy's ephemeral qualities of opacity and translucency are countered by the almost fierce materiality of the footbridge that links the administrative wing with the studios. It merges structure, space and visual orientation in a vector-like connection that cuts through the crowns of three mature chestnut trees. The presence of the white, rectangular volume amid the leaves documents Arets' sensibility to all the subtle gradients of a site in an architecture that on first impressions seems cool and hermetic.

ADDRESS Herdenkingsplein, Maastricht
CLIENT Gemeente Maastricht
BUS 1, 5, 6, 7, 24, 25 to either Kommel or Brusselsstraat
ACCESS cafeteria and lecture hall only

Limburg

Wiel Arets & Associates 1989–93

Wiel Arets & Associates 1989–93

Bonnefantenmuseum, Maastricht

The medieval city of Maastricht has undergone something of a Renaissance recently because the European Union treaty was signed there. Unlike most walled cities from the Middle Ages that were aligned on one side of a river, Maastricht's centre straddles the Maas. A new development on the east bank was made possible when the nineteenth-century Sfinx-Céramique factory decided to move from its site on the Porceleinplein. Jo Coenen, an architect based in the city, devised the masterplan for a new city quarter with housing, offices, green space and cultural facilities. He invited local and international architects to take part, which resulted in a scheme that boasts Alviro Siza, Wiel Arets and Mario Botta. The Bonnefantenmuseum, designed by Aldo Rossi, serves as the focal point in the new development's relationship to the city.

Rather than addressing the art inside, as other museum builders have done, Rossi gregariously engages the city by locating his project directly on the Maas. The Bonnefanten's 'E'-shaped floorplan has its open side to the river and is crowned by a zinc dome reminiscent of Italian architecture of the Renaissance. A panorama terrace and two steel circular stairways flank the dome, and are perhaps indicative of the site's industrial past. The entrance on the opposite side is less spectacular, except for its double-height glass doors wedged between two towers. On this side of the museum, the old factory hall by Wiebenga, a listed building that was the first reinforced concrete structure in the country, is now incorporated into the Bonnefantenmuseum. This contains temporary exhibition space on the top floor with permanent, large-scale installations on the floors below.

The first item that draws attention inside the museum is a cone-shaped lightwell where natural light illuminates the Marcel Broodthaers installation below. The public areas such as bookshop, café and library are also

Aldo Rossi 1990–92

Aldo Rossi 1990–92

also on the ground level but separate from the exhibition spaces. Moving through the building, a grand brick staircase with a skylight sweeps the visitor to the dome which is the heart of the museum. This area was intended as a working and exhibition space. The irregular fenestration of the dome, however, may attract more attention than the art itself.

Rossi's severe restraint is part of his theories on the 'analogue city', in which unobtrusive architecture highlights the vitality of the urban context in which the museum is placed. While this may be attractive to prospective clients, it leaves little excitement for the users of the building. In essence, the soberness of the floorplan and regularity of forms make the museum an open book rather than a secret envelope with hidden contents inside.

ADDRESS Avenue Céramique 250, Maastricht
PROJECT ARCHITECTS S Umberto Barbieri, G da Pozzo
CLIENT Provincial Bestuur Limburg, Maastricht
BUS 56, 57, 58, 420 to Porceleinplein (a short walk from Maastricht station)
ACCESS open; entrance fee

Aldo Rossi 1990–92

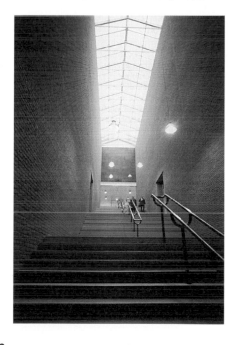

Limburg

Aldo Rossi 1990–92

De Spiegel primary school, Maastricht

An image from Sjoerd Soeters' *o1o* monograph shows children merrily at play in front of the semicircular west façade of this building. Whether this is a manipulation of our sensibilities is not clear. What is certain, though, is that the school has been designed from the child's point of view. Soeters, whose child-like affability and reputation as the 'naughtiest boy in the class' of Dutch architecture, genuinely acknowledges the needs of the young pupils, some of whom have not yet learnt to read. He decided to use a colour scheme to differentiate classrooms, which are situated in a fan-like floorplan, based on experience with similar commissions:

Sjoerd Soeters Well, I made many Kindergartens, and talking with people there I found out that it is very easy for children in a place like that to know they are the red group, or the blue group. As they cannot read yet, they can relate very strongly to colour.

Eight classrooms each have a different colour of the rainbow in their vaulted barrel roofs and trim on the doors. An auditorium sandwiched between the fan of classrooms and the staff wing uses all the colours.

Gone are the rectangular rooms and endlessly linear floorplans of older schools, and the combination of colour association and a clustered design makes a small-but-sweet project that restores faith in institutional architecture. For an architect who repeatedly references 'play' in relation to his work, Soeters delivers a school with a familiarity that would put any child at ease.

ADDRESS Sorbonnelaan 199, Maastricht
BUS 10, 21 to Sorbonnelaan
ACCESS none

Limburg

Architectenbureau Soeters 1989–92

Limburg

Architectenbureau Soeters 1989–92

Police station, Vaals

Wiel Arets considers himself a 'global' architect; a body of unique, high-standard work from his office has made him one of the few Dutch architects of international renown. One of these enigmatic designs is the police station in Vaals, a town in southern Limburg. The project arose from the reorganisation of the local police forces that necessitated a regional base for 35 staff.

Situated on the outskirts of town, the police station has nothing overtly institutional about it. A public footpath passing in front of the station gives a good view of the modest complex of three elongated volumes. The primary aim was to bridge a 6-metre drop in the terrain; it also steers visitors to the main entrance. The first volume has all the public functions, including the cells and a kennel. Staff and arrested suspects access the wing separately from below. The middle volume accommodates the officer of the watch, while the third administrative wing, made of unfinished concrete, looks over the undulating landscape. The arrest cells offer not a visual but a thematic connection to Dom van der Laan's nearby Vaals Monastery, a work which Wiel Arets admires and feels culturally close to. In an underlying irony – there the monks and here the prisoners – one of the building's themes, punishment and redemption, becomes apparent.

Clad in zinc, red cedar and raw concrete, the station's three volumes radiate an atmosphere of minimal art, an impression enhanced by their object-like placement in the landscape. Yet it would be reductive to explain Arets' work by his preference for pure geometries and natural materials. His taste for refined shades and textures that age well can be clarified in the long-term relationship a building has with its environment. To achieve this minute expression, Arets involves contractors from an early stage.

Limburg

Wiel Arets & Associates 1993–95

Wiel Arets & Associates 1993–95

FM In the presentation drawings, I noticed that there's a subtle use of colour, but in the finished buildings you only assign a subdued role to it.

Wiel Arets I'm not yet able to add strong or what I would call unnatural colours to my buildings. There is no colour in Holland. Okay, there are a few houses that are painted red like the Rietveld's Schroeder House in Utrecht, which is of course a masterpiece, but I think we are not using colour in a way that is natural. In Holland colour is used as a fashion and I am not interested in 'fashion'. I am interested in fashion. I am interested in Yamamoto and Comme de Garçons. This jacket I bought three years ago, but I also have a jacket by Yhoshi [Yamamoto] that I bought ten years ago, there is hardly a difference, it is very subtle. It is not fashion in the way people think about fashion, that changes quickly. That is not what I think architecture should be. Architecture is there for much longer.

ADDRESS Randweg, Maastrichterlaan, Vaals
DESIGN TEAM Rhea Harbers (PROJECT ARCHITECT) Delphine Clavien, Paul Egers, Michel Melenhorst
CLIENT Politieregio Limburg Zuid
BUS 54 from Maastricht station
CAR N278 to Aachen, Germany
ACCESS unless you get arrested, reception area only

Limburg

Wiel Arets & Associates 1993–95

Wiel Arets & Associates 1993–95

AZL office, Heerlen

AZL, a retirement fund for Limburg's former mining industry, commissioned Wiel Arets & Associates to convert their existing facilities, which dated from 1941. During the modernisation, the old 'U'-shaped layout of two main buildings with a connecting annex was reversed; a new wing was added with the main entrance, reception, meeting rooms and staff canteen.

The AZL office unfolds like a film script, the sheer number of details forcing movement around the building to grasp the subtlety of the spatial sequences. Arets quotes cinematography as an important influence on his work:

Wiel Arets When we design, I look strongly at how you enter the building and how you could perceive one or the other detail from different positions, the combinations you could make and the way light is entering and so on, you could say it has something of what I think has a lot to do with a filming experience. That's why I really like Jean-Luc Godard's movies, the way he shoots.

The design is serene and composed and yet offers a baroque richness of spaces, a paradox best witnessed in person. Approaching the bunker-like front elevation on Akerstraat there are two options for entering the building: either a ramp leading into the slit between the long façade and main volume, or the staircase that disappears under its protruding head. Arets suspends temporarily the traditional hierarchy, only to reconcile it later when the two paths join at the doorstep. The diverse atmospheres the building evokes are forged into a whole by these spacial techniques. A progression from the main wing, which floats seemingly weightless above the immersed parking lot, via the artificial inner yard to the back

Limburg

Limburg

Wiel Arets & Associates 1991–95

garden with its remains of the old structure shows the complex relationships which, at the same time, are increasingly discernable.

Such interplay is made possible by a fine balance between structure, programme and space. The opaque, long elevation, which appears to be mostly cantilevered, actually provides the necessary structural depth to span the parking lot. On the inside of this 'bridge' a succession of vistas through the building provides the cohesion that knits together the reception, restaurant and conference room. Arets, who exercises a tremendous scrutiny and control over the architecture, achieves this spatial coherence by continuous floorplanes. Similar to traditional Japanese architecture, he defines an interior space by the surface of the ground. When the need for a partition wall arises, the separation is realised by sliding or pivoted doors, which do not disrupt the space. Staircases are replaced by gently angled ramps that extend the spatial order vertically. This accentuation of the horizontal planes carefully metres out the possibilities of a space, without glossing over evident conflicts in the architecture.

The sobriety of the architecture finds an accomplice in the ascetic choice of materials. Large surfaces of concrete and steel charge the volumes with a dynamic checked only by distinct corner joints and glazed meeting lines. This clarity looks good and keeps attention on the basic qualities of the building. Reduced to their essential openness, the rooms find their pendant in the floating organisation of the workforce. Unlike standard office buildings where each employee has a fixed workplace, AZL uses computer technology to allow a changing daily configuration.

It speaks of Arets' intellectual rigour that vastly different themes such as internal organization, space and materials were elaborated with the same zest. The overall quality of the AZL office lies in its seductive minimalism, which reveals a complicated, multilayered life beneath. Arets

Wiel Arets & Associates 1991–95

Limburg

Wiel Arets & Associates 1991–95

explains his version of diversity: 'The fact is that we try to make buildings, which seem to be very simple, but which are incredibly rich. The richness is not developed in terms of incredible complicated shapes or details, but is expressed in a way that gives many possible interpretations'.

ADDRESS Akerstraat 92, Heerlen
PROJECT ARCHITECTS Dominic Papa,
Jo Janssen, Ani Velez
CLIENT AZL Beheer, Heerlen
GETTING THERE 5-minute walk
from Heerlen station
ACCESS public passage open
weekdays 9.00–17.00

Limburg

Wiel Arets & Associates 1991–95

Wiel Arets & Associates 1991–95

Prinsenhoek Housing, Sittard

'We do not intend to organise city life because you can't organise city life.' According to Michiel Riedijk of Neutelings Riedijk Architects, one should stick to the profession and organise the quality of the project rather than impose rules on an unpredictable urban setting. This intention comes as an understatement if one considers the architects' project for an apartment block in the southern town of Sittard.

Situated on a corner plot on a shifted junction, the Prinsenhoek block looks down towards the train station. Ignoring the council's request – which asked for a seven-storey, hockey stick-shaped building – the architects set forth and reworked the urban plan. They considered the gentrification and urbanisation of the area and the slow disappearance of the site's diverse architectural qualities. As a consequence, a villa next to the block was saved from demolition and integrated into the scheme. The block itself is organised in three layers, each articulated specifically to a theme and scale.

The base caters for the requirements of street life and has a gallery, small offices and a dental surgery. A wall of bricks hewn from Ardennes rock wraps around the plot and connects the plinth with a parking deck behind. In between it encloses a communal garden whose serene atmosphere matches that of the adjacent villa. Riedijk elaborates:

Having the garden is a very important part of the concept. Without the garden and the villa we don't have a plan; it is crucial for the integrity of the ensemble. It is tragic about modern apartment buildings that they are just dropped on the pavement. There isn't anything on the ground that generates quality.

On reflection, the charged role of the dense but slightly over-styled garden

Limburg

Limburg

Neutelings Riedijk Architecten bv 1993–95

– designed by landscape architects West 8 – holds the various elements together.

The middle section, a 'neutral block, which gives the building an urban expression' (Riedijk), holds eight, one- or two-bedroom apartments on each level which are generously served by four shafts for elevators and staircases. The block's design opens the flats on both sides without the barrier of an external gallery. Clad in dark concrete panels, the façade's 'presence of a body' is reinforced by sunken strips of windows.

Two heavily sculpted top floors form the crown of the building, which is one of the highest in the centre.

Michiel Riedijk As soon as you are on top you have a splendid view over the region. It is like living in the sky. We developed the expression of these apartments in such a way that they all have private terraces into which your neighbours cannot look. One of the things that struck us was that apartment buildings have a very homogenous quality. Let's say if you want to have an expensive apartment, luxurious could mean to live on the sixth floor but still have a very generous outdoor space for yourself.

ADDRESS Wilhelminastraat, Sittard
DESIGN TEAM Willem Jan Neutelings (PROJECT ARCHITECT) Guy Mertens, Edith Winkler, Frank Heylen, Jago van Bergen
LANDSCAPE ARCHITECTS West 8, Rotterdam
CLIENT Santiago bv, Sittard
GETTING THERE 5-minute walk from Sittard station
ACCESS none

Limburg

Neutelings Riedijk Architecten bv 1993–95

Neutelings Riedijk Architecten bv 1993–95

Rotterdam

Pathé multiplex cinema 236
Schouwburgplein 240
Bram Ladage frites stand 242
Binnenrotte Market Square 244
Blaak railway station 246
Duimdrop (licorice) box 274
De Schie penitentiary 278
Woeste Willem child daycare centre 280

Pathé multiplex cinema

Opened in March 1996, Koen van Velsen's multiplex was the finishing stone of the long-winded saga of the refurbishment of the Schouwburgplein. The cinema is, as a manager of the Pathé chain accurately described, 'the cherry on the cake of the square'. The monolithic volume does not reveal immediately the metropolitan zest that lurks behind its opaque façade. Although a cinematographic metaphor would offer itself, such a comparison is short-changing the building's ways of working. Instead of a sequence or a fixed montage, the architecture reflects what each person brings to it. The excitement of going to the cinema is embraced by the building, which subtly orchestrates a stage for the visitor's sentiment.

The size of the edifice is remarkably well-adjusted to the restrained space of the site. Although it is big it certainly does not look it. The slanted surfaces and angles of the crystalline shape are determined by the mass of seven, freely positioned auditoria and the viewlines that organise the Schouwburgplein. Unwanted edges and disturbing emergency staircases are smoothed over under translucent corrugated lexan cladding that wraps the entire structure. The lucid façade oscillates between acting as a perimeter wall and as a screen, which is in some places detached from the inner volume. A transparent glass plinth removes the twined mass from the ground and further elaborates the theme of lightweightness. The actual weight of the structure was one of the most critical design parameters because the site is located above an underground parking garage. The use of foundation pillars was restricted and a low-weight, dry-joint steel frame was employed for construction.

From the square, where the viewlines of the building generate an immediate suspense, the notion of urbanity reaches inside. The foyer moves sweepingly past the ticket counter along a grandiose staircase to the vast expanse of the hall between the hung auditoria. This expressive interstitial

Rotterdam

Architektenburo Koen van Velsen bv 1992–95

Rotterdam

Architektenburo Koen van Velsen bv 1992–95

space is the direct counterpiece to the outer appearance. The interior expands fluidly from street level and boasts a multitude of stairs, lounges and balconies luxuriously equipped with chairs by Philippe Starck. The furniture represents, along with the red carpet at the entrance and the shiny metal floor, the few timid references to the glamour of the silver screen. Yet they serve first and foremost the convenience of the general public that enjoys a drink at the bar before walking up the ramps to the theatres.

Van Velsen handles the issues associated with the public domain with maturity and elegance. The geometric shapes of the light-filled, pristine space seem to echo the idealism of the Russian constructivists. This observation does not reduce the architecture to a mere formalism, but acknowledges how the space as a medium is deployed. This multiplex radiates inner strength and conviction – if I were not an architect it would make it my ambition to become one. Yet van Velsen's overall achievement is the combination of the directness of the city with an architectural means.

ADDRESS Schouwburgplein, Rotterdam
DESIGN TEAM Lars Zwart, Gero Rutten, Marcel Steeghs, Okko van der Kam
CLIENT Pathé Cinemas, Amsterdam
GETTING THERE 2-minute walk from Centraal Station
ACCESS open

Architektenburo Koen van Velsen bv 1992–95

Rotterdam

Architektenburo Koen van Velsen bv 1992–95

Schouwburgplein

The Schouwburgplein is a spectacle, not only because of the rich materials this public platform is made of, or the gigantic street lights that hover above the square like harbour cranes. If there is really nothing going on you can drop in a gilder and adjust the position of the spotlights. The city as a stage. One day in mid March, we watched three cyclists crossing the square crash in a span of 15 minutes.

Bart Lootsma (architecture critic) That is not the design's fault, that's how it's carried out. The public space in Holland, it's not like in France or Barcelona where you can make a design and simply execute it. In Holland it is very difficult. Although it exits already so long, the Schouwburgplein is still not finished because they need to redo the epoxy floors, they were made at the wrong time of the year. So even if it was opened a couple of weeks ago, it's not finished. The lamp posts are still not working. They should have been finished two years ago, but that is not a design problem, it's a problem of the services of the city.

FM It is incomplete, it evolves and people grow accustomed to an interim solution.

BL In this case it would have been better if it would have been ready in one month. In other instances, like in Amsterdam, you have a much more historical situation and its OK when things grow in a way, but here in Rotterdam it is really the last layer in the reconstruction of the city, a kind of furnishing of the city. It would be very important from the beginning to have it there.

ADDRESS Schouwburgplein, Rotterdam
GETTING THERE 2-minute walk from Centraal Station
ACCESS open

West 8 Landscape Architects 1990–97

Rotterdam

Rotterdam

West 8 Landscape Architects 1990–97

Bram Ladage frites stand

Resembling a silver sombrero with 'Bram Ladage', the biggest name in fast food, emblazoned in blue lettering, this hilariously kitsch frites stand is the work of the normally quite subdued architect, Kees Christiaanse. Located strategically in the inner city near a shopping area, it serves frites and soft drinks to locals and visitors alike. In addition to the sombrero section, where the frites are cooked and served, there is a giant Pepsi can attached on its west side. It is used as a staffroom and storage area. Despite the obvious commercial function, Christiaanse sees the building as part of the city's urban fabric:

FM I wonder if you consider this as a piece that connects parts of the city, not as a response to a purely economic demand, but placed as a key piece making up a larger pattern.

Kees Christiaanse This was a very conscious design because it stands in the Lijnbaan by Bakema which is a monument of urbanism. If you accept this is a monument of urbanism, then you also directly say that anything that is standing in that pedestrian area cannot be a building. It would be an object which is standing there; it should be detached to be more like an object standing on the pavement like a sculpture. There would be no building that is referring in material or something else to the surrounding. In that respect it relates very much to the character of the landmark.

ADDRESS Binnenwegplein, Rotterdam
PROJECT ARCHITECTS Kees Christiaanse, Chiel van der Stelt
METRO to Churchillplein
TRAM 3 from Centraal Station
ACCESS open

Rotterdam

Kees Christiaanse Architects and Planners 1992

Kees Christiaanse Architects and Planners 1992

Binnenrotte Market Square

This is not your typical market square: the first time I saw it, I thought it was an art installation. On this huge plane, symmetrical rows of blue light emanate from stainless steel cabinets that seem placed for aesthetic rather than practical reasons. They turn out to be electricity generators for the 500 market stalls that occupy the square twice weekly. Binnenrotteplein is the result of the demolition of an overground nineteenth-century railway line. Now replaced by a tunnel, the destruction of this outdated infrastructure allowed the city to regain a vast amount of precious space.

West 8's design borders the fantastically retro Rotterdam Blaak station (page 246) and Piet Blom's cubical-shaped houses, both architectural landmarks in the city, and lives up to its historically impressive counterparts. A large void provides the backdrop for a *mise en scène*, which is really performed by its users. The market square slopes gently southwards from Blaak station and is only broken up by the electrical generators and five slim street light poles. As an estimated 70,000 people use the square each market day, it was logical that West 8 chose to rely on real life rather than built drama to animate the work, and as such Michel de Certeau's theory of the urban walker providing the atmosphere of the city is fitting for this project.

ADDRESS Binnenrotteplein, Rotterdam
TRAIN to Blaak from Centraal Station
METRO Blaak
TRAM 1, 3 from Centraal Station
ACCESS open

Rotterdam

West 8 Landscape Architects 1988–95

Rotterdam

West 8 Landscape Architects 1988-95

Blaak railway station

Train stations are the most public of buildings and the architectural department responsible for designs is Nederlandse Spoorwegen (NS) Engineering, part of Dutch Railway.

In 1993, the elevated railway tracks that made Rotterdam look like Chicago on the Maas were demolished and moved to a tunnel under the city. The barrier-razing effect liberated valuable land in the city centre and connected the Kop van Zuid with its neighbouring districts.

Entirely submerged, Blaak station marks its presence above ground with a large, saucer-shaped canopy. The most impressive aspect of the architecture or, rather, its absence, is under the canopy: here a gigantic hole reveals the tracks 40 metres below Binnenrotteplein. The station and its void have been conceived as an oversized duct to release the powerful air currents and build up of pressure produced by passing trains. If not dealt with, the currents would knock passengers off their feet! Although this opening has its architectural merits, the NS management would never have agreed to the additional costs if there was not a case for such an extravaganza. In the interior, a cascade of escalators descends to the scooped-out platforms. Here Dutch artist Peter Struycken has developed a light installation to give the cavity a less threatening character. NS had in mind a 'Caribbean atmposhere', but you can just as well imagine being in an atomic fall-out shelter in the Seychelles.

ADDRESS Binnenrotteplein, Rotterdam
DESIGN TEAM M Haring, L Vákár
TRAIN southbound trains from Centraal Station
METRO Blaak
TRAM 1, 3 from Centraal Station
ACCESS open

Rotterdam

Harry C H Reijnders 1987–93

Rotterdam

Harry C H Reijnders 1987–93

Boijmans van Beuningen Museum extension

The Boijmans van Beuningen Museum is one of the oldest and most important visual-arts institutions in The Netherlands. The original building, designed by A van der Steur in 1935, was expanded 20 years ago by A Bodon who, in 1991, was also responsible for the plan which positioned the bookshop and café by the main entrance on the Mathenesserlaan. Hubert-Jan Henket's extension was completed in the same period and is an example of close cooperation between the architect and Wim Crouwel, then director of the museum. Although purpose built to house the museum's van Beuningen-de Vriese collection of nearly 10,000 pre-industrial implements and utensils, the new wing also serves as a space to exhibit twentieth-century industrial design and crafts.

The extension replaces what was once a terrace at the end of a 250-metre axis which runs from a pond to an obelisk in the museum garden. Henket's transparent box addresses nature, incorporating the greenery into the museum experience. In order to control the flood of daylight, the architect designed a large overhanging roof, which protrudes 2 metres beyond the façade with steel slats extending a further 2 metres. Horizontal strips under the slats filter direct sunlight and protect precious works.

To reduce the amount of surface area taken up by the appendage, Henket divided the pavilion into two floors. The newly acquired collection and workrooms are located in the windowless basement while on the level above pieces are exhibited using natural light. In essence, then, the project becomes like a sculpture on a plinth. Like Henket's extension to the Teylers Museum in Haarlem (see page 80), this design involves little intrusion into the existing structure.

It will be interesting to see what happens in the future, as the Boijmans

Rotterdam

Hubert-Jan Henket Architecten bv 1989–91

Hubert-Jan Henket Architecten bv 1989–91

van Beuningen Museum is yet again looking to expand, this time under the supervision of the dynamic new director, Chris Dercon. He has chosen the Belgian partnership of Robrecht and Daem to design the museum's newest extension. The Boijmans Museum may be seen as exemplifying the Dutch attitude towards architecture: working firmly within contemporary culture but always looking toward the future.

Rotterdam

ADDRESS Mathenesserlaan 18–20, Rotterdam
PROJECT ARCHITECT Hubert-Jan Henket
TRAM 4, 5 from Centraal Station
ACCESS open; entrance fee

Hubert-Jan Henket Architecten bv 1989–91

Hubert-Jan Henket Architecten bv 1989–91

The Netherlands Architecture Institute

Situated on the northern edge of the Museum Park in Rotterdam, The Netherlands Architecture Institute serves as both a boundary and an integral element of the cultural centre of the city. Only a short walk from the Boijmans van Beuningen Museum, Jo Coenen's imposing structure is also neighbour to the Museum of Natural History and OMA's Kunsthal. The high pergola of the NAI finds its contextual reference in the tower of the Boijmans van Beuningen Museum. Coenen's plan also contributes to the urban fabric of the square: a public route through its central hall serves as a connection from the Museum Park to a traffic artery.

Its primary function, though, is to preserve and document The Netherlands' rich architectural and urban-planning heritage, serving as a research centre for local and international designers, members of the arts community, and the general public. The NAI invites them to engage in an ongoing discourse around contemporary architecture and design.

The competition brief for the institute asked six invited architects to articulate the various programmes of the NAI – library, exhibition hall, archives, and offices – through separate volumes. Coenen's scheme consists of four distinct elements: a central reception hall with entrances from the north and south, a glass box suspended in an exoskeletal frame, a brick-faced exhibition hall, and a curved wing clad in corrugated steel, resting on concrete columns. These disparate elements are skillfully held together by a glass transport house containing a central staircase and lifts.

The long arched body on the north end of the site, a massive elevated structure, houses the archives and research centre of the Institute and serves as a backdrop to the public spaces, which are set back from the street by a pond on the south side. Grounded in the water, the rotated entrance building containing the lecture hall and café intersects the glass box with library and reading room, in turn creating a lightweight volume

Jo Coenen & Co Architekten 1988–93

Rotterdam

Jo Coenen & Co Architekten 1988–93

in which the foyer is hung. Coenen's design, with its repeated use of suspended volumes, is a strategy which results in a building that appears rather closed from the street but in fact unfolds from the inside, establishing elegant visual connections among interior and exterior spaces.

The purity of the suspended bridges and galleries finds its repercussions in the absence of plaster ceilings, laying bare all the service lines. Equal attention has been directed toward external elements of the site such as the concrete threshold, the pond, and the waterside terrace, which not only unify the site but also transform the pond from a merely decorative addition to an demarcation of an environment which one enters when visiting the Institute. The result is a subtle monumentalism. Situated within the pond, Auke de Vries's gigantic sculpture, in which steel forms seem tenuously balanced, gives a vertical prospect to the static surface of the water. The columns of the pergola represent the architects' reluctance to use closed structures. On opposite ends of the archive wing are the Coenen café and the editorial offices of the monthly magazine *Archis*.

ADDRESS Museum Park 25, Rotterdam
CLIENT Stichting Beheer Onroerend Goed/The Netherlands Architecture Institute
GETTING THERE METRO, TRAMS 4 and 5, BUS 32, or 15-minute walk from Centraal Station
ACCESS 10.00–17.00 Tuesday to Saturday, 11.00–17.00 Sunday and public holidays (tel (0)10–4401200)

Jo Coenen & Co Architekten 1988–93

Jo Coenen & Co Architekten 1988–93

Kunsthal

The Kunsthal, a temporary exhibition gallery, resolutely refuses to adopt the role of an art institution. At a time when the imperative of beauty is crumbling, OMA's architecture can be seen as a *pièce de résistance* of contemporary culture against clichéd aesthetic dogma. Liberated from stylistic idiom, the Kunsthal is widely accessible to a general audience. The building, which at first seems so roughly made, on closer inspection turns out to be full of anecdotal references. It is a parody of another temple to the fine arts: Mies van der Rohe's Neue Nationalgallerie in Berlin. Yet it does not get stuck in a postmodern litany but rushes forward to ambush the unsuspecting visitor with a array of materials, montages and an euphoric zest for living in the city. The casual pragmatism that pervades this spectacle drags Miesian elegance into the profanity of Holland.

A box-like volume, with a different material at every corner, the Kunsthal is organised around a system of spiralling ramps. They tie exhibition halls, public functions and administrative offices into a dense architectural promenade that culminates on the roof. The awkwardly located site is bounded to the south by the Westzeedijk, a main thoroughfare, and the Museumpark to the north. These entirely supplementary conditions are interwoven by a pedestrian route leading to the street and a service road at the bottom of the slope. The design incorporates these axes in a pedestrian ramp that cuts the building into two differently sized segments. Denying architectural conventions, the main entrance is tucked away halfway through the public passage. From here one enters the foyer-cum-auditorium, whose slanted floor steers up to the first of two large exhibition halls in the eastern section. Concrete columns emerging at a right angle from the inclined ground inject the reality of a parking garage into the cultural building. This intrusion of motifs from everyday life is rounded off by the view from the bookstore's horizontally cut-out

Rotterdam

Office for Metropolitan Architecture 1987–92

segment. The lowered floor allows visitors to look ahead into the space of the café beneath. This creates an unsettling out-of-body experience as one sees the underside of the storey on which one is positioned.

Ascending to the first hall, the path bifurcates as a staircase departs for the uppermost gallery and the roof garden. Hall 1's connection to the lower Hall 2 is twofold: either via a small gallery along the eastern perimeter, with a steel-grating floor providing a vertigo-inducing view to the ground, or via a ramp that descends along the original point of entry. The paying visitor is divided from the common man and woman by a fully glazed wall that allows them to observe each other with slightly embarrassed glances. At the bottom, a black ceiling sets the dark tone of Hall 2. In a surreal displacement, the columns are made of tree trunks that continue the grid of the Museumpark outside. At night the ghostly reflection of these structural trees expands the space endlessly. The most *outré* impression is provided by the moment the bark of the trunk swings open like a door, revealing electrical wires inside.

In the gallery on top, next to the pear trees of the roof garden, the tilted columns of the foyer below shoot through the floor, impairing one's sense of balance in the process. The Kunsthal is packed with these alienating attributes. Although the polemic of the building borders on the demented, it never strays from the path of sanity. It is actually a very serious and intelligent design.

ADDRESS Westzeedijk 341, Rotterdam
CLIENT Gemeente Rotterdam
DESIGN TEAM Rem Koolhaas, Fuminori Hoshino
TRAM 5 fom Centraal Station to Museumpark
ACCESS open; entrance fee

Office for Metropolitan Architecture 1987–92

Office for Metropolitan Architecture 1987–92

Museum of Natural History extension

In the lumbering shadow of the Kunsthal sits the Museum of Natural History. Once the residence of Hoboken, the Villa Dijkzigt, a neo-classical building from 1851, has housed the Natuurmuseum for some years. To increase exhibition space and to step up the profile of the institution as part of the refurbishment of the Museumpark by OMA, the popular office of Erik van Egeraat was commissioned to restore the villa and create an extension. The resulting appendage is clad entirely in glass, which acts like a layer of skin above a steel structure and a concrete block that holds the new exhibition space. Waves of daylight enter this box through a 1.5-metre slit in the structure. The remainder of the extension holds a library and offices. An obvious comparison can be drawn with its neighbour on the other end of the Museumpark, Jo Coenen's NAI (see page 252), with its centrally featured glass-clad box.

Van Egeraat dismantled the old façade of the villa, placing a wall behind the entrance to the Natuurmuseum, which serves to unite the old with the new. The extension is internally connected to the villa via two glass footbridges. Van Egeraat's extension must be respected for its clarity and precision and because it does not try to overshadow the original museum, but exists in harmony with it. Unfortunately for the museum, it seems that some visitors only experience the extension from the glass coffee shop of the Kunsthal located opposite.

ADDRESS Westzeedijk, Rotterdam
PROJECT ARCHITECT Erik van Egeraat
TRAM 5 from Centraal Station
ACCESS open

Erik van Egeraat Associated Architects 1993–96

Rotterdam

Rotterdam

Erik van Egeraat Associated Architects 1993–96

Erasmus Bridge

The Erasmus Bridge is possibly as close an architect in Calvinist Holland will get to realising trophy architecture. Of the three competing proposals for a bridge linking the former harbour district of Kop van Zuid to the centre of Rotterdam, van Berkel and Bos's asymmetric design was the most flamboyant and expensive. The decision of the city council to go along with the 139-metre-high single pylon signalled its commitment to the evolving urban district on the south bank of the Maas.

In the six years from conception until the bridge was opened, the traditionally divided roles of architect and engineer were effectively blurred. The placement of the pylon in front of the Noordereiland between Nieuwe Maas and Koningshaven follows the urbanistic viewpoint that relates its centre of gravity towards the new city quarter. Subsequently the two separate waterways differentiated the deck into a suspended and a hinged section which can be lifted hydraulically for oversized vessels. The deck's elegant curve contrasts with the sculpted mast while leaving the view of the waterfront intact.

In the early design stage, the pylon was conceived as a freestanding concrete element, an idea that was quickly abandoned because of unpredictable static and technical difficulties. In the final version it is stiffened by four tension cables in the back, forming a triangle which sits on two massive pillars sticking out from the bed of the Maas. The forked pylon tweaks its way from the horizontal into the vertical where the play of bending moments freezes it in a delicate balance between the pulling cables of the deck and its own weight. The plasticity of the conflicting forces reveal the critical ramification of van Berkel and Bos's method, which utilises structural properties to refine their architecture.

Two of the world's largest offshore cranes were required to assemble the prefabricated steel members and to lift the completed structure into

Van Berkel & Bos Architecten bv 1990–96

Rotterdam

Van Berkel & Bos Architecten bv 1990–96

place. This spectacle of marine engineering was only surpassed by the panic that broke out when shortly after the opening ceremony, the deck's suspension cables started to swing ferociously in foul weather. Apparently, strong gales of wind kept the rainwater from rinsing off the cables, which began to vibrate from the additional load. Although the fault was the engineers', the architects had to bear the brunt of the public embarrassment. A temporary solution was found by crossbracing the cables with a series of giant bands that limit their movement to a minimum.

In spite of this incident, the Erasmus Bridge, with its thoroughly modelled tectonics, excels. The stunning number of carefully crafted fixings, handrails and landscape elements on the surface of the bridge makes the architects' attitude towards materials literally palpable. Every detail underwent the scrutiny of an omnipresent dynamic that leaves no angle straight or surface even. This dynamism comes alive when the hydraulic section is lifted. The direction of the waterway intersects the bridge's trajectory at an angle of almost 70 degrees. Viewing the 60-metre-long ramp from the deck as it describes a smooth arc into the sky, it appears as if this chunk of steel were twisted by an invisible earthquake.

Yet the architects' resources were not fully exhausted by such an impressive fusion of structure and event. The colour of the Erasmus bridge, which on overcast days blends in with the grey of the clouds, is at night transformed into a shimmering blue that delays its earthbound weight, setting it afloat above the dark water of the Maas.

ADDRESS Erasmus Bridge, Rotterdam
GETTING THERE METRO to Wilhelminaplein, TRAM 5 from Centraal Station, or a 10-minute walk from Centraal Station
ACCESS open

Van Berkel & Bos Architecten bv 1990–96

Van Berkel & Bos Architecten bv 1990–96

Kop van Zuid

The phasing out of the old harbour area and the correlating construction of the container port a few kilometres down the Maas gave the city of Rotterdam the opportunity to rethink the role of its centre. Located close to downtown, the former docks left by the move had all the qualities needed to become the new urban centre of gravity. This potential was recognised by Riek Bakker, then director of Rotterdam Town Development. In 1987 Teun Koolhaas Associates were commissioned to draw up a masterplan for the Kop van Zuid, while Norman Foster was chosen to make a proposal for the Wilhelminapier stretching west. By 2004 this programme will accommodate a massive 5000 dwelling units, 380,000 square metres of offices, 50,000 square metres of leisure, and 3500 square metres of retail. This effort is equalled by large-scale infrastructural intervention that includes the extension of the metro network to the south, as well as bus and tram connections via a new river crossing. The design is orientated along the lines of square city blocks that organise the ground in a linear grid. The volumes of the apartment blocks are sculpted to adapt to the open spaces of the river and the basins. This strategy is similar to Jo Coenen's plan for the KNSM island in eastern Amsterdam (see page 50), employing monumental architectural scale in order to synthesise a character for the peninsula.

The opening of the Erasmus bridge (see page 262) was a major step towards the full integration of the Kop van Zuid into the city. It changed Rotterdam's mental geography: the river is no longer a boundary but a unifying element. The landmark character of van Berkel and Bos's bridge points to the other theme that gave form to the urban design: the notion of cityscape. The urban presence of the buildings is a direct result of the regulations laid down in 'quality books'. They defined the project's objectives in terms of urbanism, public space and programmatic intentions.

Teun Koolhaas Associates, Foster Associates 1987– 97 (first phase)

Rotterdam

Rotterdam

Teun Koolhaas Associates, Foster Associates 1987– 97 (first phase)

The rough volumetric shape was then elaborated in a series of progress meetings between architects and a panel of supervisors. The quality team (including Hans Kollhoff, Frits van Voorden, Dick van Mourik, Bernard Huet, Joan Busquets, and Hans Wittermans) met four times a year to discuss and refine the developing architecture.

The first buildings in place give a good impression of what Kop van Zuid will look like. The Wilhelminahof office complex (on Wilhelmina-plein) opposite the Erasmus Bridge anchors the new neighbourhood in the administrative landscape of Rotterdam. The block consists of two sections: the court of law by Rob Ligtvoed of Kraaijvanger Urbis and the tax and customs service by Cees Dam and Partners. Big excavations from the slab frame the entrance of the new metro station. This civic centre forms the threshold to the Wilhelminapier, where heavy construction has yet to begin. The pier is still dominated by the remnants of the dock industry, including the former headquarters of the Holland America Lijn. Recently renovated, it is now home to the Hotel New York, one of the most enjoyable eateries along the Maas.

Two apartment buildings stand out from the housing that has been finished so far. Along the Louis Pregerkade, Frits van Dongen casts a truly urban programme into three expressively terraced perimeter blocks. The wedge-like volumes contain more than 600 dwellings, a crèche, and a sports club with six tennis courts. The recreational functions are hidden from the view of the street. The introverted appearance is compensated by a public plaza between two of the blocks. The other project of merit is CEPEZED's semi-circular apartment building along Stiltjestraat. The design successfully integrates an existing structure into the new layout, and gives its immediate surroundings a strong spatial cohesion in the process. The external access galleries face into the courtyard, which

Teun Koolhaas Associates, Foster Associates 1987– 97 (first phase)

Teun Koolhaas Associates, Foster Associates 1987– 97 (first phase)

emphasises the communal quality of the building. The project's most distinct feature is the timber-clad, staggered façade, which enlarges the floor area of the apartments. The amount of detailing and the warm quality of the materials exemplify CEPEZED's ability to diverge from the slick technical solutions they so often apply in their work.

The next wave of construction is already under way. It will include a college by Erik van Egeraat Associates and the competition-winning Luxor theatre by Bolles Wilson, who are also authors of the landscaped waterfront around the Wilheminakade. One is left somewhat uneasy by the sheer size of the project. The sophistication of the architecture is not matched by the open spaces between the blocks. The monumental scale seems to suggest that the success of the area will be found in the urban qualities of the architecture rather than generating diversity on the street level. The fact that the streetscape is left to few, if beautifully designed, elements indicates that it has yet to develop a life of its own. At a symposium on cityscape in the Jan van Eyck Academy in Maastricht, Susan Buck Morse noted that the technological ecstasy of cityscapes overwhelms one's sensory apprehension and rises above the understandable; it becomes sublime – an observation that also applies to the Kop van Zuid.

ADDRESS Wilheminapier and surroundings, Rotterdam
INVITED FIRMS include Frits van Dongen/de Architekten Cie, van Berkel and Bos, CEPEZED, Kraijvanger Urbis, Cees Dam and Partners, Bolles Wilson, Erik van Egeraat Associates
METRO to Wilhelminaplein
ACCESS open

Teun Koolhaas Associates, Foster Associates 1987– 97 (first phase)

Rotterdam

Rotterdam

Teun Koolhaas Associates, Foster Associates 1987– 97 (first phase)

Bridge-keeper's house

Positioned close to the southern tip of the Erasmus Bridge, Bolles Wilson's design offers a welcome relief from the large-scale buildings of the Kop van Zuid. The reduced size of the building ties in cleverly the flat prospect of the Maas and the upshooting Wilhelminahof on the other side of the street. The bridge-keeper's house supervises and operates the hydraulic section of the bridge, hence the awkward shape protruding over the river.

In addition to the organisation of the ship traffic, it is one in a series of landscape elements that structures the waterfront. A few metres away a panoramic catwalk starts that gives a splendid view of the Erasmus Bridge. It is not without irony that it takes a public podium properly to witness the vertical exuberance of van Berkel and Bos's showpiece of engineering.

Rotterdam

ADDRESS Wilhelminakade, Rotterdam
METRO to Wilhelminaplein
ACCESS public bridge only

Architekturbüro Bolles Wilson 1994–96

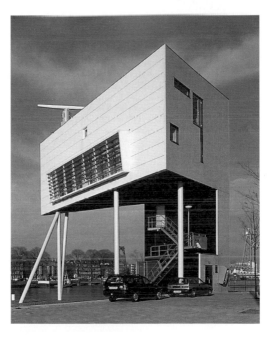

Rotterdam

Architekturbüro Bolles Wilson 1994–96

Duimdrop (licorice) box

This box, the most rudimentary of all architectural forms, exists for the storage and distribution of toys for children aged from 4 to 11 from the local community, most of whom are foreigners to The Netherlands. Because their families often need to send money back to their home countries, toys are not a priority. This project aims to alleviate this situation. Basic toys are signed out by an attendant who mans the box at specified hours. The more desirable toys are borrowed in return for 'duimdrop money', which is earned by doing small jobs in the neighbourhood. The boxes first appeared in 1993 when six containers were placed on public squares in Rotterdam. Joost Glissener, the young architect responsible for the boxes' design, explains:

FM It's a fantastic idea. Who though of it?

Joost Glissener This guy – a social worker – came to me because I had done a children's restaurant. He said we want to do something to lend toys on a square in a city and it has to be built in serial production. We start with six containers and if it's a success, there will be more. So I had to make something that was quite easy to repeat and which was quite abstract as a form so that it could fit in every location. The first idea of the social worker was to make a big pedestal.

KB Like a plinth?

JG Like a fairytale house. Something like that. I was thinking if you've seen it once it's getting boring. Such a direct form. I wanted to make an object that was not only fun for kids, but good to see for other people. It has to last for at least five years on the same spot without falling apart. So I proposed to use the container.

The boxes are recycled containers adapted to store toys and are equipped

Joost Glissener 1993–95

Joost Glissenr 1993–95

with a lavatory and kitchen facilities for the duimdrop attendant, who is usually a volunteer or an unemployed person. The graphic 'duimdrop lettering' attracts attention and lends the box an advertising feel. Steel grills protect the wooden material of the containers from violent actions and graffiti. The entire structure glows from within at night, giving it a mysterious quality.

The project is successful for its simple and functional design, and on a social level because of its impact on the community. The boxes represent an intelligent and successful experiment, and their temporary nature adds to the unique feeling of the project.

ADDRESSES (a selection) Burgemeester Hoffmanplein, BUS 32 to Noordereiland; Rosestraat, BUS 66 to Rosestraat; Tidemanstraat, TRAM 1, 7 to Mathenesserplein
COST NFL 35,000 per box
ACCESS open at specified hours

Joost Glissener 1993–95

Rotterdam

Joost Glissener 1993–95

De Schie penitentiary

This building was one of our favourite sites along the train route on our almost daily excursions to Rotterdam. Its sleek and colourful appearance and location on the periphery of the city recall Ikea stores and giant shopping centres. Unfortunately, the building's function is much more serious. It is a penitentiary designed by Carl Weeber with the help of Dutch artist Peter Struycken, who often collaborates with architects on public buildings (see pages 246 and 284).

Although the brief was specific (it wanted to restrict the movements of users), and at times even restrictive and unpleasant, Weeber wanted to use colour to counteract its character. The resulting windowless 80-metre façade in orange and blue faces the canal, while Struycken's interior colours are also exuberant. According to the artist the colours remind inmates, 90 per cent of whom are from warmer climes, of their homes.

Peter Struycken [Weeber] proposed to give every cell a colour, and because he is colourblind he asked me to design the colours. I think he's the architect most interested in colour that I know and he's colourblind. I designed six colours, one of which was rejected because it was considered stigmatising. The ministry really couldn't have an argument why they shouldn't apply colour to the cells so the five colours were randomly put in the cells. Carel wanted all the walls and the ceiling painted. Each cell has a window which looks into the courtyard so the light reflection is very intense. In the end they liked it and now coloured cells are used in other prisons too.

ADDRESS Professor Jonkersweg 7, Rotterdam
BUS 32 from Churchillplein
ACCESS none (unless you are serving time)

Rotterdam

De Architecten Cie/Carel Weeber 1985–87

Rotterdam

De Architecten Cie/Carel Weeber 1985–87

Woeste Willem child daycare centre

Prinsenland, a new district in east Rotterdam, is a low-density garden suburb with lawn-framed streets and cosy dwellings. Although the invited architectural firms produced some noteworthy projects, the neighbourhood gives an impression of permanent bliss. The streets and dwellings do not have the capacity to develop the urban diversity so typical of Rotterdam. But the people seem to be perfectly happy living in such a predictable, if unexciting, environment. Along with CEPEZED's design for a child daycare centre, other projects by Kees Christiaanse (Barcode building, Jacques Dutilhweg and timber villas, Jimnah-singel), DKV (Office Volkswoningen, Prins Alexanderlaan) and Mecanoo (Ringvaartplasbuurt Oost, near Jacques Dutilhweg) are noteworthy.

The kindergarten by Jan Pesman makes the most of the restricted site by incorporating the outdoor area in the grid of the building's tubular steel structure. The nomadic character of the modular system gives it an unthreatening, protective appearance. The exoskeletal frame is based on 5-metre-wide units from which all elements are hung. The box of the daycare centre is clad in blue glass panels with alternating window strips, which are at ground level for toddlers and further above for adults. In this way the modest size of the two-storey building is cloaked. At its southern end the volume is cut off diagonally by a glass façade that blurs the division between inside and out. The transition is buffered by roof modules that also give shade in the summer. The industrial hardness of the engineering solution is only softened by a hedge on the perimeter that masks the playground from the public sphere.

ADDRESS Ben Goerionstraat 6, Rotterdam
METRO to Schenkel BUS 190 from Hofplein
ACCESS none

Rotterdam

CEPEZED 1992–93

CEPEZED 1992–93

Zuid Holland

'De Struyck' student housing, The Hague 284
City Hall and Library, The Hague 288
Service tunnel, The Hague 292
De Resident, The Hague 294
Haagse Bos office tower, The Hague 298
Haagse Poort Building, The Hague 302
Dedemvaartweg housing festival, The Hague 306
Beelden aan Zee Museum, Scheveningen 312
Rijswijk station and railway tunnel 314
Open-air theatre, Delft 316
Anne Frank Primary School, Papendrecht 318

'De Struyck' student housing, The Hague

'De Struyck' refers to Peter Struycken, the artist who collaborated with Carel Weeber on this and many other projects (see page 278). Struycken, who chose the wall colours for part of the Groninger Museum, is one of the best-known artists in The Netherlands. He explained how the building came to be named after him: 'Because the first design I made for it was very detailed, all in green and white, it looked like a bush. And when my name is pronounced, it means bush. So he [the designer] associated it with my name. And he said a building should have a name'. Because the architect is colourblind, Struycken was called in to design the flame-like skin of the 20-storey building. Although the pattern appears red, it is in fact varying shades of green, black and white bricks with red mortar.

KB And how did you change from the green palette to the rose?

Peter Struycken That was a decision of Carel [Weeber]. Carel wanted a red building. I think he had seen one he liked in India. And he asked me to think of a tiling structure that would fit into the red building. When you look at it you see the green and the white and the black of the tiles. But when you photograph it's not possible. Because of the confusion of the red and the green the photographic material can't catch up. Like a person who's colourblind and can't decide between red and green.

The ground floor has shops and office space. Above this the transition from public to private areas takes place, with the ascending floors used for university student accommodation. Each room is based on a studio plan, with living, eating, studying and bathroom facilities. The same

Zuid Holland

De Architecten Cie/Carel Weeber 1992–96

Zuid Holland

De Architecten Cie/Carel Weeber 1992–96

floorplan, of 20 flats per floor, is repeated on each storey. Double-height windows along the north-west corner are lit in varying colours, providing a spectacle at night.

ADDRESS corner of Bontekoekade/Rijswijkseplein/Rijswijkseweg, The Hague
PROJECT ARCHITECT Carel Weeber
CLIENT Chr. Woningbouwvereniging Patrimonium Den Haag/nv Stedelijk Belang Den Haag
COST NFL21 million
GETTING THERE 2-minute walk from Hollandse Spoor station
ACCESS ground floor only

Zuid Holland

De Architecten Cie/Carel Weeber 1992–96

De Architecten Cie/Carel Weeber 1992–96

City Hall and Library, The Hague

Richard Meier's style is unmistakable: Ozymandias-scaled gleaming white buildings that express the pristine coldness of corporate power. Prestigious projects all over the globe, including his new $billion headquarters for the Getty Foundation in California, have secured Meier the legendary status of American counterparts such as Philip Johnson and I M Pei. His hulking building in the inner city of The Hague is no exception. Located on the corner of two main streets, the building is wedged into a site 275x80 metres and includes a council chamber, marriage hall, public library, municipal offices, leasable offices and shop fronts. Monumental and intimidating, it commands the attention of passers-by. It is part of the renewal scheme of the city and is one of the first built examples of what will encompass an entirely new downtown area.

A semicircular floor plan on the north-west corner of the site houses the library and leads to an entrance area with shops and café. From here a visitor continues to the heart of the building, the awe-inspiring, 12th-floor, light-filled atrium. Here visitors can lounge on benches, view an exhibition detailing plans for the redevelopment of the downtown area or present themselves at a reception desk. Municipal offices are housed in the strips of the wings enclosing the atrium. Freestanding transparent elevators link these floors, providing a gradual transition between public and private space. Walkways connecting the two wings are not for the faint hearted. Try to walk across the pedestrian bridge on the 12th-floor – the vertiginous sensation can turn legs to jelly.

A glass roof is supported by columns of laminated wood and includes a sun-deflecting surface which helps to control overheating on sunny days. Because it was necessary to allow plenty of sunlight to hit the atrium floor Meier and Gunter Standke balanced the size of the windows accessing direct sunlight with indirect lighting by means of reflection. The

Zuid Holland

Richard Meier & Partners Architects 1986–95

Richard Meier & Partners Architects 1986–95

whitewashed steel of the lift cores and walkways in the atrium also serve to deflect some of the light.

Although the building's size is a bit alienating, it manages successfully to combine a variety of programmes. Although rather loathe to admit it, I did enjoy sitting in the atrium watching the *mise en scènes* on the floors above where civil servants mix with couples about to be married, and corporate waiters steer their indispensable coffee trays. The atrium is the ultimate place for the voyeur, while privacy is limited to the offices behind closed doors. The pleasure that an individual finds is meagre, however, in comparison with the effect a building of this proportion has on The Hague.

ADDRESS Spui/Kalvermarkt, The Hague
PROJECT ARCHITECT Rijk Rietveld
DESIGN TEAM Richard Meier, Gunter Standke
CLIENT Algemeen Burgerlijk Pensioenfonds Project Management Grabowski & Poort, The Hague
TRAM 8, 10 from Hollandse Spoor station, 6 from Centraal Station
ACCESS library and atrium only

Zuid Holland

Richard Meier & Partners Architects 1986–95

Richard Meier & Partners Architects 1986–95

Service tunnel, The Hague

Never before, as Rem Koolhaas notes in *S,M,L,XL,* has 'an arbitrary section of road been bombarded by a single office with so much architectural consideration as the Spui (the sluice) in The Hague by OMA'. Right in the centre of town, Koolhaas' office realised their ground-breaking National Dance Theatre, conceded defeat as they were refused the commission for the equally arresting City Hall after having won the competition, and now literally have gone underground. The Hague is engulfed in a construction frenzy that will create a new city centre with an additional 500,000 square metres of space for its administrative and commercial sectors. It will be accompanied by a restriction of individual vehicle access to the centre, while around the demarcated zone a buffer of underground car parks will absorb the extra traffic. A cornerstone of this development is OMA's service tunnel beneath the Grote Marktstraat.

This spectacular urban intervention combines a tram tunnel, two stations at each end and a submerged car park above. Throughout its length of about a kilometre the touching points of the different modes of transport are made visible by transparent divisions. Pedestrian ramps cut through the double-storey parking layer and establish visual connections with the traffic and tram line below. The directness of these encounters and the destabilised, heterogeneous space makes the service tunnel the extruded equivalent of the Piranesian space that OMA envisioned for Lille's high-speed train station.

ADDRESS Grote Marktstraat, The Hague
DESIGN TEAM Rem Koolhaas, Rients Dijkstra, Rene Heijne
CLIENT The Hague
TRAM 8, 10 from Hollandse Spoor station, 6 from Centraal Station
ACCESS open

Zuid Holland

Office for Metropolitan Architecture 1990–99

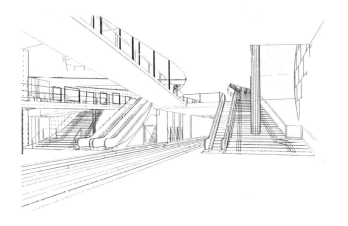

Office for Metropolitan Architecture 1990–99

De Resident, The Hague

Early next century there will be an entirely new city centre in The Hague. Hans van Dijk, critic for the journal *Archis,* asked: 'A new centre, ... does The Hague actually have an old centre?' It is easy to see van Dijk's point: there is little civic life in the cathedral or public squares, and The Hague sprawls aimlessly, Los Angeles-like, but without its flare or style.

In 1988 it was decided that the centre would be rebuilt. The new development was meant to stretch from Grote Marktstraat, the main shopping boulevard, to Centraal Station. Also included was a plan to build over the Utrechtsebaan motorway, so countering its barrier effect. The Haagse Poort (page 302) by Kraaijvanger Urbis is one of the first buildings of this part of the plan; Benthem Crouwel's high-rise office building (page 298) is another; while further along buildings by Zwarts and Jansma, part of the Grotiusplaats complex, will also straddle the highway.

De Resident is the new development between the Herengracht and Turfmarkt, a site originally known as AgFi after the proposed Ministry of Agriculture and Fishing. Originally, Sir Norman Foster was chosen to draw up the masterplan for the site but, because of budgetary constraints, Rob Krier was chosen instead.

In 1991 *Rijksbouwmeester* (government architect) Kees Rijnboutt and The Hague alderman Peter Noordanus held a workshop to refine the urban proposal. Gunnar Daan, Bert Dirrix, Peter Drijver and Sjoerd Soeters were participants, and all are now constructing on the site. Since then they have been joined by Karelse van der Meer, Adolfo Natalini, Michael Graves and Cesar Pelli.

Rigorous guidelines have led some to criticise Krier's masterplan. Because he believes that public space should be squeezed out of an amorphously conceived urban block, building lines are sacred and the architects do not have much room for change. Krier stipulated that: flat roofs

Rob Krier (masterplan) 1988–2005

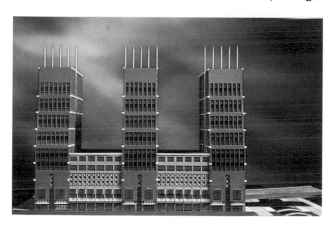

Zuid Holland

Rob Krier (masterplan) 1988–2005

were taboo and there should be no protruding balconies; dark bricks must be the main material; the tops of the buildings should have recognisable features while keeping the traditional hierarchy of basement–middle–crown; and there should be a separate entrance accessible directly from the public space. Unsurprisingly, the over-prescriptive solution is a postmodern utopian approach that does not allow much creativity.

None of the architecture, at least from the drawings and rendered images, is very exciting. Each building, however, does embody the character of the individual practice responsible for the design. Michael Graves, of Disney fame, has made a conversion of the Transitorium that has two overpowering gabled roofs. Soeters' contribution is a building with shops and a car park on the corner of the Turfmarkt-Zwarteweg. Three vertical slabs dominate the upper portion of the building while the tram tunnel captivates the viewer's attention at ground level. Cesar Pelli's Zürich tower is the most expressive and was inspired by the artist Naum Gabo. Pelli has created a building that expresses itself through a green metal cap. Working maquettes showed various 'hair styles' that could be put on the building.

De Resident has been criticised by many, but only when the public lives in and around the new centre will it be possible to judge the scheme.

ADDRESS Turfmarkt and surroundings, The Hague
ARCHITECTS Gunnar Daan, Bert Dirrix, Peter Drijver, Michael Graves, Karelse van der Meer Architecten, Rob Krier, Adolfo Natalini, Cesar Pelli, Sjoerd Soeters, CH & Partners
TRAM 8, 10 from Hollandse Spoor Station, 2, 3, 6, 7 from Centraal Station
ACCESS open

Rob Krier (masterplan) 1988–2005

Zuid Holland

Rob Krier (masterplan) 1988–2005

Haagse Bos office tower, The Hague

The Dutch, who have had to reclaim 70 per cent of their land from the sea, have an unsentimental if cunning view of land use. Even with so much reclaimed land, the country is still the second most densely populated country in the world (after Japan), yet it does not seem overcrowded. One explanation could be the Dutch manner of intensifying the use of land rather than spreading out horizontally. This logic suggests that only a multiple-layered building type, with a cross section that stacks traffic infrastructure, shops, offices or dwellings will prevent cities such as Rotterdam or The Hague from collapsing under their own congestion.

The Hague plans another large-scale upgrading of a neighbourhood near Rob Krier's De Resident urban-renewal scheme (see page 294). The Bezuidenhout quarter is cut off from the city centre by the submerged Utrechtsebaan motorway. The council commissioned Spanish architect Joan Busquets (of Barcelona fame) to draw up a masterplan that would soften the existing barrier condition while also providing 60,000 square metres of additional office and retail space. The central strategy of Busquet's plan is partially to cover the road with a series of open squares that will be anchored by public functions and institutions. In the most daring gesture three medium-rise office buildings span the trench of Utrechtsebaan as a series of inhabited bridges.

The first and most impressive of these buildings is Benthem Crouwel's 19-storey office tower that straddles the motorway on the edge of Haagse Bos, a large park that is also home to the Royal Dutch Palace. The site allowed only a minimal building footprint on the edge of the motorway below. This constraint determined a binary structural system, whose sections were elaborated individually. The load-bearing concrete skeleton in the east and west façades is stiffened by externally mounted steel beams which give the building a commanding technical expression. The peculiar

Benthem Crouwel Architecten bv 1993–96

Zuid Holland

Zuid Holland

Benthem Crouwel Architecten bv 1993–96

bridge-like layout turned the usual programmatic sequence of an office building upside down. Hovering above the road, the entrance hall is intersected by the angled struts of the concrete truss that support the base of the tower. Above the foyer are five levels of parking, a double-storey section with a restaurant and a congress venue, and 12 levels of office space.

This hybrid composition becomes most elegantly manifest in the west elevation, which succumbs to the functions' seductive aesthetic. The access ramps of the parking decks protrude from the volume and disrupt its orthogonal symmetry in the process. Throughout the office levels on top, the glass façade recesses from the massive steel tubes outside. This interstitial space is filled on every third level by a small terrace giving employees a resting area while allowing them to enjoy the view of the park. In this addition to an otherwise domineering architecture, Jan Benthem's and Mels Crouwel's concern for a human scale becomes evident. The tower relates the size of the façade to the needs of the users, and so unexpectedly gains in stature.

ADDRESS Bezuidenhoutseweg 10/12, The Hague
CONSULTANTS Ove Arup and Partners
DESIGN TEAM Andre Bekker, Jacob Borren, Cees van Giessen, Roy van Rijk
CLIENT Multi Vastgoed bv
BUS 43 from Centraal Station
ACCESS foyer only

Zuid Holland

Benthem Crouwel Architecten bv 1993–96

Zuid Holland

Benthem Crouwel Architecten bv 1993–96

Haagse Poort Building, The Hague

This massive building straddles the Utrechtsebaan motorway that leads into The Hague. As cars zoom by workers above sip coffee and deal with their daily tasks. The 60-metre arch acts as a gateway to the city, a fact that Nationale Nederlanden, the insurance corporation occupying the building, capitalises on in its publicity material. Offices for 2700 staff are accommodated in the 270-metre complex, which consists of one central corridor to which parts are attached. All facilities – elevators, stairs, toilets, conference rooms, reception and computer rooms – are located along this spinal element that connects the high-rise building on the eastern side of the motorway to the western low-rise section, which contains three wings placed at right angles. The greenish cladding of the corridor section is actually ceramic: it is attached specially so that the tiles will not blow off in adverse weather conditions.

Communal space is allocated to each floor, with rooms that can be reserved for meetings. There are private dining rooms catered for by an in-house service. In addition, a dining hall on the eighth floor with a capacity for 700 people boasts a magnificent view of the city. (Conscious that all government agents and official visitors enter the city via the arch, the architects deliberately avoided placing the restaurants for fear of associating them with motorway service stations.) 'The Diamond', a smaller 200-seat restaurant, is named after the 23-metre dome at top. The dome has giant screens to block the heat of the sun by moving a convenient roller system.

The building took 36 months to complete and was done in phases: first the tower, then the lower rise and finally the arch. Made of specially prefabricated parts that fit perfectly, the arch has two 60-metre circle-shaped steel arches with load-bearing construction hidden in the two end walls. It is clad with glass on the bottom, but the windows can only be

Kraaijvanger Urbis 1990–91

Zuid Holland

Zuid Holland

Kraaijvanger Urbis 1990–91

cleaned when it rains because the water droplets from the cleaners would distract drivers and could cause accidents.

The cool veneer and corporate attitude is sensed immediately on entering the reception area, but like most large-scale multinationals the edifices they create serve their corporate aims rather than those of the general public.

ADDRESS Beatrixlaan/Schenkkade, The Hague
PROJECT ARCHITECT Rob Ligtvoet
INTERIOR ARCHITECT Kees Moerman, Kraaijvanger Urbis
LANDSCAPE ARCHITECT Kirsten Mastenbroek, Kraaijvanger Urbis
CLIENT Nationale Nederlanden/Vastgoed, Den Haag
GETTING THERE 5-minute walk from Hollandse Spoor station
ACCESS none

Zuid Holland

Kraaijvanger Urbis 1990–91

Zuid Holland

Kraaijvanger Urbis 1990–91

Dedemvaartweg housing festival, The Hague

Throughout the late 1980s and the early 1990s, before it became *de rigueur* for international trade magazines to highlight the work of Dutch architects, the country's housing production enjoyed a comparatively high standard. The tradition of large housing corporations mostly subsidised by the public sector guaranteed a consistent architectural quality. A showcase festival in The Hague was organised to celebrate the occasion of the 200,000th dwelling built since the post-war reconstruction boom. The festival, along the Dedemvaartweg to the west of the city, invited many of the top architectural firms to participate. Their display projects and model estates explored the possibilities of urban dwelling types, and the fruits of their labours can be seen all along the street, conveniently identified and dated by commemorative plaques.

In the northern section Kas Oosterhuis experimented with a building type that has no windows to the street. The inhabitants of the bungalow are screened off from the public realm by a 3-metre-high translucent fence of corrugated plastic. Planned as a model for a low-rise, high-density urban context, it focuses on the enclave of the courtyard. Next door is the contribution of Mecanoo Architecten, an office best known for their use of elegant materials. They tackle the same assumption of a kasbah morphology, but derive a different solution. Instead of turning inward, their design employs the garage as a plinth that transforms the living quarters to a *piano nobile* overlooking the street. The well-honed geometry of the volumes oozes a luxury that stands in sharp contrast with the social implications of its typology.

Located further down the road is the site earmarked for two proposals by Zaha Hadid and Bernard Tschumi that unfortunately were never built. Their place was taken by a group of seven offices that have their youth

Zuid Holland

various architects 1988–97

Zuid Holland

various architects 1988–97

as a common denominator. Most noteable is MVRDV's Walled-In House. Project architect Nathalie de Vries paraphrased a new modality of city life in a combination of the hyper-private and hyper-public. The converse characteristics are articulated by a hermetic brick wall that wraps the bedrooms and the terrace on the first floor, and a partially glazed plinth that holds the sitting area below. The floorplans reveal an engagement of the different spheres that diverges from the above-mentioned projects. The private domain is literally inserted in the transparent base, resulting in a complex internal sequence that links indoor and outdoor spaces.

The most innovative project is Kees Christiaanse's and Aart Zaaijer's apartment block on plot 25. The architecture indicates their fondness for a constructivist aesthetic, one that stages a spatial tension through an interplay of surfaces and volumes. The large, excavated voids are the result of the different access typologies that penetrate the slab. This absence is filled with the vitality of communal areas that serve as a buffer between the intimacy of the apartments and the surrounding city.

FM There is a certain change from the Dedemvaartweg in comparison to the more recent atrium house in Nieuwegein. Both times you work with access patterns to make it an experience for the people, but at the same time it has become more sober.

Kees Christiaanse The building in the Dedemvaartweg is special because the whole area started as a housing festival and therefore we had more facilities. The buildings at Nieuwegein are for the free market, which means the building in The Hague looks better, but the Nieuwegein is much better in terms of doing the job for money, it is very special that you are able to realise such a thing in the market housing.

FM I would not say that one is better than the other. I found both of them

Zuid Holland

various architects 1988–97

very precise in their solutions but I found The Hague more open ... now that you tell me there were economic reasons.

KC Maybe I can say that if we would have made the Nieuwegein building at the time we did The Hague, maybe we would not have made the two slabs out of one colour brick, but we would have used different planes of material. In that sense we are becoming more reduced, maybe.

KB Because of the budget?

KC No, conceptually.

ADDRESS Dedemvaartweg, various plots: corner of Melis Stokelaan, The Hague
INVITED FIRMS (selection) Kees Christiaanse Architects and Planners 1988–92, Mecanoo Architecten 1989–92, MVRDV 1995–97, Oosterhuis Associates 1989–92
TRAM 8, 9 from Hollandse Spoor station
ACCESS public areas only

various architects 1988–97

Zuid Holland

various architects 1988–97

Beelden aan Zee Museum, Scheveningen

When the Scholtens, who had been collecting art for their whole lives, decided to bequeath over 650 sculptures to a museum, they discovered that no institution could show more than a fraction of the work. Dismayed by the idea of works put into storage, they decided to make their home a museum. The intrusion proved too much, but the idea inspired the building of a purpose-built environment on a site under and around a nineteenth-century pavilion by the sea at Scheveningen.

Paul Scholten, brother of one of the collectors and now director of the museum, explained how Wim Quist was the only architect considered based on his reputation as the Dutch 'museum builder'. Quist's solution to a complicated site was to build a museum in the sand dunes. It proved problematic as the removal of sand from the site was prohibited, and the task of shifting several tons of sand on-site was very expensive and time-consuming.

The lack of a façade creates a hidden treasure effect on entering the building. A ticket area and café lead to the first of the two main semicircular gallery spaces, where the juxtaposition of concrete, steel and sandstone with the huge space bathed in natural light from above results in an ethereal feeling of serenity. Many routes can be chosen between the outside and inside. The interior is also linked by a corridor to a fabulous exterior of patios and a dramatic ramp that double as exhibition spaces.

ADDRESS Harteveltstraat 1, Scheveningen, The Hague
DESIGN TEAM H Korver, P Meeuwise
COST NFL12 million
BUS 22 from Scheveningen station to Kurhaus
ACCESS Tuesday–Sunday 11.00–17.00 (tel. (31) 703 584050)

Zuid Holland

Architektenburo Quist bv 1990–96

Zuid Holland

Architektenburo Quist bv 1990–96

Rijswijk station and railway tunnel

The cliché, 'the wrong side of the tracks', like all hackneyed expressions, has some truth in it. Most suburban towns are severed by transport lines which are problematic in design matters because they cut into valuable public space. Rijswijk, a suburb of The Hague, was previously cut in two by the railway line through the centre of town. The design team from Nederlandse Spoorwegen (the Dutch National Railway), led by Harry Reijnders, is working to modernise these modes of transport by devising new systems that claw back land from these parts of the city. Such a plan has been put into action in Rijswijk and the prospect of regaining a large amount of public space in the centre of town is inspiring and exciting.

The railway line, which divides the inner city into disparate elements, was to be widened to four lines. The increased number of trains passing through Rijswijk ruled out a surface solution, and so the station and tracks have been moved underground. The result is that vital space and the interconnections between formerly separated neighbourhoods in the centre of town have been reclaimed. The giant pyramid is the entrance to the station where passengers descend to await the trains, much like the solution found at Rotterdam Blaak station (see page 246). At street level the pyramid is echoed by six smaller ones that lead the pedestrian through a new urban piazza. At the far end is a new development with domestic and commercial units that seeks ideologically to connect with the 1950s housing blocks that once stood on the opposite side of the tracks.

ADDRESS Rijswijk station
TRAIN south-bound trains from Hollandse Spoor station
ACCESS open

Zuid Holland

Harry C H Reijnders 1994–96

Zuid Holland

Harry C H Reijnders 1994–96

Open-air theatre, Delft

This open-air theatre, which resembles a Charles Eames chair but of gargantuan proportions, was one of MVRDV's first projects. The discreet design cleverly unites the disparate concerns of the community, its landscape and local politics. The brief called for a playground for 12–16 year olds: a difficult task even under normal circumstances and accentuated further by the problems of the area.

After discussions with local schools, MVRDV devised a combined openair theatre and basketball field, attempting to combine three elements: the domestic shell that invites users to hang out; the landscaped dykes that lead to the auditorium from the surrounding bicycle and pedestrian routes; and the basketball field, which serves a utilitarian function for adolescents. The shell was made using an experimental technique that tested the limits of the medium that Winy Maas proposed for another project while working for OMA. Four layers of concrete make the extremely thin shell (just 16 centimetres) and act as laminated plywood, allowing complete flexibility in the shape of the structure.

The theatre – now neglected and full of graffiti – has never been officially opened to the public because of debates between the client, contractor, and director. Although seemingly problematic and insignificant in the light of MVRDV's bigger commissions, the theatre illustrates how politics and community can effect the outcome of a modest design.

ADDRESS Abtswoude Park, Delft Zuid
DESIGN TEAM Winy Maas, Jacob van Rijs, Nathalie de Vries
TRAM 1
BUS 62, 63, 64 to Ghandi Laan
ACCESS open

Zuid Holland

MVRDV 1992

Zuid Holland

MVRDV 1992

Anne Frank Primary School, Papendrecht

Once you meet the principal and caretaker of the Anne Frank School in Papendrecht, one thing is clear: they are proud of the building that they fought to erect and are happy with their choice of architect. Herman Hertzberger designs important and large-scale public commissions in The Netherlands, but it is his humanitarian approach to architecture (grand theatres, art centres, libraries and schools) that sets him above his colleagues. Perhaps the most significant characteristic of Hertzberger's work is his innovative approach to communal spaces in buildings. In this project for a small primary school, a central open space on the ground floor serves as a meeting area for the children and doubles as an auditorium or theatre, with a short stack of stairs acting as a proscenium. From this central area students can go to the cloakroom, classrooms or physical education room.

A staircase from the side of the 'stage' wraps around the building and acts as a suspended balcony for the first and second floors. Emphasis on visual links here is repeated throughout the building. On the higher levels are more classrooms, while the staff rooms are at the top.

Throughout the project the architect has employed inexpensive materials to cut costs and has focused instead on design issues and although built with an extremely small budget, Hertzberger retains his flare for the theatrical with the dramatic central void.

ADDRESS Rozenstraat, Papendrecht
CLIENT Gemeente Papendrecht
BUS from Papendrecht station
ACCESS only by appointment

Zuid Holland

Architectuurstudio Herman Hertzberger 1992–94

Zuid Holland

Architectuurstudio Herman Hertzberger 1992–94

Index

The Netherlands: a guide to recent architecture

Academy of Fine Arts (Maastricht)
210–212
Adema, Jerôme 146
Adviesburo voor Bouwtechniek 166
Ajax museum (Amsterdam) 56
Alberts & van Huut
    GasUnie Building **116–118**
    International School of Amsterdam **60**
Alberts, Ton 60, 116, 182
Alessi 96
Almelo 132
Almere 86
Amersfoort 8, 178–182
Amstelveen 62
Amsterdam 16–68
Amsterdam Arena **56–58**
Andersson, Sven-Ingvar 26
Anne Frank Primary School
    (Papendrecht) **318**
Apartment tower, Laan Corpus den
    Hoorn (Groningen) **112**
Apeldoorn 144–146
Archis 6
Arets, Wiel 182, 220, 222
    Academy of Fine Arts **210–212**
    AZL OFFICE **224**
    Police station **220–222**
Armstrong-Law, Margaret 60
Artoteek (Breda) **190**
Asselberg, Frans 8
Atelier Mendini
    Groninger Museum **96–100**
Augé, Marc 56

Bakker, Riek 8, 172, 266

Baljon, Lodewijk 134
Barbieri, S Umberto 216
Barcode building (Rotterdam) 280
Bates, Gary 166
Beelden aan Zee Museum (Scheveningen)
    312
Bekker, Andre 300
Benthem Crouwel Architecten bv 294
    De Pont Foundation **198**
    Haagse Bos office tower **298–300**
    Ibis Hotel and Wagon Lits **20**
    Museum Nieuwland (polder museum)
        90
    Schiphol Airport Terminal West, World
        Trade Centre and Plaza **64–68**
    Tivoli parking garage **200**
Benthem, Jan 20, 66, 68, 300
Berg, Kirsten van der 174
Berkel, Ben van 8, 54, 134, 178
Berlage, H P 50, 52
Bezaanjachtplein housing (Amsterdam)
    42
Binnenrotte Market Square (Rotterdam)
    244
Bjoeks climbing hall (Groningen) **122**
Blaak railway station (Rotterdam) **246**
Blom, Piet 244
    Russian Palace (Amersfoort) **182**
Boijmans van Beuningen Museum
    extension (Rotterdam) **248–250**
Bolles Wilson 270
    Bridge-keeper's house **272**
Bonesmo, Gro 104
Bonnefantenmuseum (Maastricht)
    214–216

BOOM Environmental Consultants 32
Booth, Mike 156
Borneo Sporenburg urban development (Amsterdam) **46–48**
Borren, Jacob 300
Bos, Caroline 8, 54, 178
Bosch Haslett
Bezaanjachtplein housing **42**
Bosch, John 42
Bram Ladage frites stand (Rotterdam) **242**
Branson Coates Architects 68
Breda 190–196
Bridge-keeper's house (Rotterdam) 272
Brockmeier, Guus 68
Brouwer, Alex 76
Bruijn, Willem 78, 142
Busquets, Joan 268, 298
Buy, Tilly 124
Buys en Van der Wijst Interieur 80
Byzantium (Amsterdam) **24**

Castricum 84
Centraal Station (Amsterdam) 20
CEPEZED 268–270
Woeste Willem child daycare centre **280**
Chasse Theatre (Breda) **192–194**
Child daycare centre (Soest) **184–186**
Christiaanse, Kees 24, 48, 170, 180, 242, 280, 308–310
Bram Ladage frites stand **242**
GWL terrain **28–32**
Koekoeksweg housing **180**
Rembrandthage apartments **170**
City Hall and Library (The Hague) **288–290**

Claus en Kaan Architecten 48
Eurotwin Business Centre **38–40**
Landsteinerlaan housing **114**
Claus, Felix 38, 40, 112
Clavien, Delphine 222
CoBrA Museum (Amstelveen) **62**
Coenen, Jo 214, 266
Netherlands Architecture Institute, The **252–254**
Piraeus apartment block **50–52**
Coop Himmelb(l)au 98
Copijn Groenadviseurs Utrecht 118
Cornubert, Christophe 166
Crimson 172
Crols, Evert 162
Crouwel, Mels 20, 66, 68, 300
Crouwel, Wim 248

Daan, Gunnar 294
De Hunze boathouse **102**
Fries Museum **124**
Dam, Cees 268
De Architect 6
De Architecten Cie
De Schie penitentiary **278**
'De Struyck' student housing **284–286**
Stadsschouwburg De Harmonie **126**
De Architectengroep 48, 156
Housing and shops **140**
De Hoep visitor centre (Castricum) **84**
De Hoge Veluwe 148
De Hunze boathouse (Groningen) **102**
De Pont Foundation (Tilburg) **198**
De Realiteit (Almere) **86**
De Resident (The Hague) **294–296**

De Schie penitentiary (Rotterdam)
278
De Spiegel primary school (Maastricht)
218
'De Struyck' student housing (The Hague)
284–286
Dedemvaartweg housing festival (The
Hague) **306–310**
Delft 316
Dercon, Chris 250
Didyk, E 148
Dijk, Hans van 294
Dijk, J van 148
Dijk, Walter van 176
Dijkstra, Rients 128, 172, 174, 292
Dirrix, Bert 294
DJ&V Architecten
Child daycare centre **184–186**
DKV Architecten 32, 280
Döll, Henk 132
Dongen, Frits van 268
Stadsschouwburg De Harmonie **126**
Driessen, Roeland 158
Drijver, Peter 294
Duimdrop box (Rotterdam) **274–276**
Duivesteijn, Adri 8

Ede 142
Educatorium (Utrecht) **164–166**
Eelman, Richard 166
Egeraat, Erik van 260, 270
Museum of Natural History extension
260
Egers, Paul 222
Enschede 134

Erasmus Bridge (Rotterdam) **262–264**
Erve, Paul van der 42
Eurotwin Business Centre (Amsterdam)
38–40

Faculty for Economics and Management
(Utrecht) **168**
50/10kv distributing substation
(Amersfoort) **178**
Fire station (Breda) **196**
Foster Associates
Kop van Zuid **266–270**
Foster, Sir Norman 294
Fries Museum (Leeuwarden) **124**

Gabo, Naum 296
GasUnie Building (Groningen) **116–118**
Geuze, Adriaan 46, 48
Giessen, Cees van 300
Glissener, Joost 76, 148
Duimdrop box **274–276**
Gortemaker, Roelof 68
Grabowski & Poort
Amsterdam Arena **56–58**
Graham, Dan 164
Grassi, Giorgio
Public Library **108**
Graves, Michael 294, 296
Groenewoud, Gerard 124
Groningen 96–128
Groninger Museum **96–100**
GWL terrain (Amsterdam) **28–32**

Haagse Bos office tower (The Hague)
294, **298–300**

Haagse Poort Building (The Hague) **302–304**
Haarlem 80
Hadid, Zaha 306
Hamfeldt, Burton 162
Harbers, Rhea 222
Haring, M 246
Haslett, Gordon 42
Heat Transfer Station (Utrecht) **176**
Heerlen 228
Heeswick, Hans von
Artoteek **190**
Heijne, Rene 292
Henket, Hubert-Jan 80, 250
Boijmans van Beuningen Museum
extension **248–250**
Teylers Museum extension **80**
Herk, Van & De Klein 48
Hertzberger, Herman 144, 192
Anne Frank Primary School **318**
Chassé Theatre **192–194**
Herzog & de Meuron 48
Heuvel, Dirk van den 142
Hilversum 72
Hoenderloo 148
Höhne & Rapp 48
Holl, Steven 48
Holzer, Jenny 66
Hoshino, Fuminori 258
Hotel New York (Rotterdam) 268
Houben, Francine 150
House of Fine Arts (Apeldoorn) **144–146**
Housing (Huizen) **78**
Housing and shops, Gerard Noodtstraat
(Nijmegen) **140**

Huet, Bernard 268
Huizen 78
Huut, Max van 60, 116, 182

Ibis Hotel and Wagon Lits (Amsterdam)
20
Ingenieursburo Linssen 166
Ingenieursburo Wassenaar, Haren 100
International School of Amsterdam **60**
Isala College (Silvolde) **150**

Janssen, Jo 228

Kaan, Cees 40, 112, 114
Kam, Okko van der 238
Klaasse, K 176
Klok, Arjan 174
Kloosterboer, Wim 46, 48
Koekoeksweg housing (Amersfoort) **180**
Koetsier, Tiemen 146
Kollhoff, Hans 268
Piraeus apartment block **50–52**
Koolhaas, Rem 8, 24, 72, 104, 166, 258,
292
Koolhaas, Teun 86
De Realiteit **86**
Kop van Zuid **266–270**
Koolhaas, Tomas 24
Kop van Zuid (Rotterdam) 262, **266–270**
Korver, H 312
Korver, Lilian 110
Kraaijvanger Urbis 268, 294
Haagse Poort Building **302–304**
Krier, Rob 298
De Resident **294–296**

The Netherlands: a guide to recent architecture

Kroller–Mueller Museum 148
Kruunenberg, Gerard 42
Kunsthal (Rotterdam) 256–258
Kurokawa, Kisho 26
    Van Gogh Museum extension 26

Laan, Dom van der 220
Laarhoven, Henk van 80
Landsteinerlaan housing (Groningen) 114
Le Corbusier 158
Leescafé 108
Leeuwarden 124–128
Leidse Rijn urban development 172–174
Lelystad 90–92
Library (Zeewolde) 88
Liemburg, Ton 90
Ligtvoed, Rob 268
Ligtvoet, Rob 304
Linnemann, M 176
Löhmann, H 198
Lootsma, Bart 104, 202, 240
Lucchi, Michele de 98
Luxor theatre (Rotterdam) 270

Maas, Winy 34, 36, 72, 148, 154, 156, 316
Maastricht 212–218
Magni, Marco 106
Makkink, Rianne 128
Mani, Victor 92
    Sportmuseum 92
Mark, Arno van der 52
Martella, Gaetano 106

Mastbroek, Bjarne
    Housing and shops 140
    Two-family house 154–156
Mastenbroek, Bjarne 48
Maurer, Ingo 120
Max. Architectuur Stedenbouw
    Leidse Rijn urban development 172–174
    Ugliest house in The Netherlands, The 128
Mecanoo Architecten bv 280, 306, 310
    Faculty for Economics and Management 168
    Isala College 150
    Public Library 132
Meer, Karelse van der 122, 294
Meeuwise, P 312
Meier, Richard 8, 288
    City Hall and Library, The Hague 288–290
Meijer, Harry 16
Melenhorst, Michel 222
Mendini, Alessandro 96
Mendini, Francesco 100
Meyer & Van Schoten 32
Mies van der Rohe, Ludwig 256
Min 2 Produkties
    De Hoep visitor centre 84
Min, Maarten 84
Minnaertgebouw (Utrecht) 160–162
Moehrlein, Johannes
    Bjoeks climbing hall 122
Moerman, Kees 304
Mourik, Dick van 268
Mulder, Arjan 76, 148
Museum Nieuwland (polder museum)

(Lelystad) **90**
Museum of Natural History extension
  (Rotterdam) 260
MVRDV 6, 142, 308, 310
  Open-air theatre **316**
  Porter's Lodges **148**
  Two-family house **154–156**
  VPRO head office **72–76**
  WOZOCO **34–36**

NACO
  Schiphol Airport Terminal West, World
    Trade Centre and Plaza **64–68**
Nagelkerke, Cees 110
  Rode Weeshuisstraat housing **110**
Natalini Architetti
  Shops, apartments and offices,
    Waagstraat **106**
Natalini, Adolfo 106, 294
National Dance Theatre (The Hague) 292
Nationale Nederlanden 302
Nederlandse Spoorwegen Engineering
  246
Neeltje Jans Water Pavilion
  (Oosterschelde) **202–206**
Netherlands Architecture Institute, The
  252–254
Neutelings Riedijk Architecten bv 6, 30,
  32, 48
  Fire station **196**
  Housing (Huizen) **78**
  Minnaertgebouw **160–162**
  Prinsenhoek Housing **230–232**
  Print workshop **142**
Neutelings, Willem Jan 78, 142, 162, 232

New Metropolis (Amsterdam) **16–18**
Nieuwegein 170
Nijmegen 140
Nio, Maurice 206
NL Architects
  Heat Transfer Station **176**
Noordanus, Peter 294
Nooyer, Olaf de 16
NOX Architecten
  Neeltje Jans Water Pavilion **202–206**

Office for Metropolitan Architecture 8,
  48, 120, 126, 160, 260, 316
  Byzantium **24**
  Educatorium **164–166**
  Kunsthal **256–258**
  Service tunnel **292**
  Toilet **104**
Office Volkswoningen (Rotterdam)
  280
Olaf, Erwin
  Toilet **104**
OMA, see Office for Metropolitan
  Architecture
Onwuka, Chidi 162
Oosterhuis Associates 310
Oosterhuis, Kas 306
  Neeltje Jans Water Pavilion **202–206**
Oosterschelde 206
Open-air theatre (Delft) **316**
Osdorp (Amsterdam) 34
Ostinelli, Roberto 98
Otonomo Architecten
  'Vos Maupertus' interior design
    superstore **120**

The Netherlands: a guide to recent architecture

Otterlo 148
Oud, J J P 132
Ove Arup and Partners 300

Papa, Dominic 228
Papendrecht 318
Pathé multiplex cinema (Rotterdam)
   236–238
Pelli, Cesar 294, 296
Pesman, Jan 280
Piano, Renzo 16
   New Metropolis **16–18**
Piet Hein Tunnel (Amsterdam) **54**
Piraeus apartment block (Amsterdam)
   50–52
Pol, Liesbeth van der 30, 44, 48
   Twiske West residential neighbourhood
   44
Police station (Vaals) **220–222**
Porter's Lodges, Park Hoge Veluwe
   148
Pozzo, G da 216
Prinsenhoek Housing (Sittard) **230–232**
Prinsenland (Rotterdam) 280
Print workshop (Ede) **142**
Public Library (Almelo) **132**
Public Library (Groningen) **108**

Quist, Wim 26, 62, 312
   Beelden aan Zee Museum **312**
   CoBrA Museum **62**

Rapp, Christian 48
   Piraeus apartment block **50–52**
Realiteit (Almere) 86

Reijnders, Harry C H
   Blaak railway station **246**
   Rijswijk station and railway tunnel
   314
Rembrandthage apartments (Nieuwegein)
   170
Riedijk, Michiel 32, 78, 142, 162, 196,
   230, 232
Rientjes, Ronald 112
Rietveld, Gerrit 28, 154, 222
Rietveld, Rijk 290
Rijk, Roy van 300
Rijksmuseum (Amsterdam) 26
Rijksmuseum Twenthe (Enschede)
   134–136
Rijnboutt, Kees 294
Rijs, Jacob van 36, 72, 148, 156, 316
Rijswijk station and railway tunnel
   314
Rijzenburg 148
Ringvaartplasbuurt Oost (Rotterdam)
   280
Riquois, Sebastiaan 48
Robrecht and Daem 250
Rode Weeshuisstraat housing
   (Groningen) **110**
Roorda, Ruurd 170
Rosmalen, Teresa van 80
Rossi, Aldo
   Bonnefantenmuseum **214–216**
Rotterdam 8, 236–280
Rotterdam Blaak station 244
Rozenstraat 318
Russian Palace (Amersfoort) **182**
Rutten, Gero 238

Sandberg, Willem 62
Scelsi, Nazario 106
Schendel, Mark 128
Scheveningen 312
Schijf, Gerard 100
Schilder, Gerrit 78
Schiphol Airport Terminal West,
    World Trade Centre and Plaza
    64–68
Schippers, K 142
Scholten, Paul 312
Schouwburgplein (Rotterdam) **240**
Schrauwen, Corinne 106
Schroeder House 154
Schuurman, Rob
    Amsterdam Arena **56–58**
Service tunnel (The Hague) 292
Seumern, Willem van 110
Shops, apartments and offices,
    Waagstraat (Groningen) **108**
Silvolde 150
Sittard 232
Sjoerd Soeters architectural office
    (Amsterdam) **22**
Slotboom, Kees 170
Soest 184–186
Soeters, Sjoerd 56, 58, 82, 294, 296
    De Spiegel primary school **218**
    Sjoerd Soeters architectural office
        22
    Zandvoort Circus (amusement centre
        and cinema) **82**
Sportmuseum (Lelystad) **92**
Spruybroek, Lars 206
Staalenhoef, A 198

Stadsschouwburg De Harmonie
    (Leeuwarden) **126**
Standke, Gunter 288
Starck, Philippe 98, 120, 238
Steeghs, Marcel 238
Steiner, Ron 24
Steiner, Rudolf 60
Stelt, Chiel van der 242
Steur, A van der 248
Streets, etc
    Almelo
        Het Baken 132
        Stadhuisplein 132
    Almere, Realiteit 86
    Amersfoort
        Haussmanstraat 182
        Koekoeksstraat 180
        Molierestraat 182
        Smallepad 178
        Sprecuwenstraat 180
    Amsterdam
        Bezaanjachtplein 42
        Burgemeester Stramanweg 58
        Coehornerhoek 44
        Cornelius van Eesterenlaan 54
        Kerkstraat 22
        KNSM Laan 52
        Leidseplein 24
        Museumplein 26
        Nesserhoek 44
        Ookmeerweg 36
        Paperveerweg 40
        Paulus Potterstraat 26
        Reimerswaalstraat 36
        Sandbergplein 62

The Netherlands: a guide to recent architecture

The Netherlands: a guide to recent architecture

Streets, etc
    Schipholweg 68
    Spoortslaan 60
    Stadhouderskade 24
    Stationsplein 20
    Van Hallstraat 32
    Van Hogendorpstraat 32
    Zuider IJdijk 54
Apeldoorn, Nieuwmanstraat 146
Breda
    Boschstraat 190
    Claudius Prinsenlaan 194
    Tramsingel 196
Castricum, Zeeweg 84
Ede, Maxwellstraat 142
Groningen
    Bieskemaar 122
    Concourslaan 118
    Donderslaan 114
    Grote Markt Noordzijde 106
    Guldenstraat 106
    Laan Corpus den Hoorn 112, 120
    Landsteinerlaan 114
    Museumeiland 100
    Oude Boteringestraat 108
    Raedinussingel 102
    Rode Weeshuisstraat 110
    Waagstraat 106
Haarlem, Spaarne 80
Heerlen, Akerstraat 228
Hilversum, Sumatralaan 76
Huizen, Hardwijkerzand 78
Leeuwarden
    Okkingastate 128
    Ruiterskwartier 126

Turfmarkt 124
Lelystad
    Museumweg 92
    Oostvaardersdijk 90
Maastricht
    Avenue Céramique 216
    Herdenkingsplein 212
    Sorbonnelaan 218
Nijmegen, Gerard Noodtstraat 140
Papendrecht, Rozenstraat 318
Rotterdam
    Ben Goerionstraat 280
    Binnenrotteplein 244, 246
    Binnenwegplein 242
    Burgemeester Hoffmanplein 276
    Jacques Dutilhweg 280
    Jimnahsingel 280
    Kop van Zuid 272
    Louis Pregerkade 268
    Mathenesserlaan 250
    Museum Park 254
    Prins Alexanderlaan 280
    Professor Jonkersweg 278
    Rosestraat 276
    Schouwburgplein 236, 238, 240
    Tidemanstraat 276
    Westzeedijk 258, 260
    Wilhelminakade 272
Scheveningen, Harteveltstraat 312
Silvolde, Laan van Schuylenburch 150
Sittard, Wilhelminastraat 232
Soest, Talmalaan 186
The Hague
    Beatrixlaan 304
    Bezuidenhoutseweg 300

Streets, etc
  Bontekoekade 286
  Dedemvaartweg 308, 310
  Grote Marktstraat 292, 294
  Herengracht 294
  Kalvermarkt 290
  Melis Stokelaan 310
  Rijswijkseplein 286
  Rijswijkseweg 286
  Turfmarkt 294, 296
  Tilburg
    Veemarkt 200
    Wilhelminapark 198
  Utrecht
    Archimedeslaan 158
    Koningslaan 156
    Leuvenlaan 162, 166
    Padualaan 168
    Rembrandthage (Galecop Nieuwegein) 170
    Rijksstraatweg 176
  Vaals
    Maastrichterlaan 222
    Randweg 222
  Zandvoort, Gasthuisplein 82
  Zeewolde, Kerkstraat 88
Struycken, Peter 98, 246, **278**, 284

Taut, Bruno 148
Team 4 Architecten
  Groninger Museum **96–100**
Teeuwen, Claire 120
Teylers Museum extension (Haarlem) **80**
The Hague 284–310
Tilburg 198–200

Timmer, Willem 76
Tivoli parking garage, Tilburg **200**
Toilet (Groningen) **104**
Transitorium (The Hague) 296
Tschumi, Bernard 306
Twiske West residential neighbourhood
  (Amsterdam) 44
Two-family house (Utrecht) **154–156**

Uehara, Yushi 48
University of Utrecht 160
Utrecht 8, 154–168, 176
Uytenhaak, Rudy 144
  House of Fine Arts **144–146**

Vaals 220–222
Vaals Monastery 220
Vákár, L 246
Van Berkel & Bos Architecten bv 48, 182
  Erasmus Bridge **262–264**
  50/10kv distributing substation
    (Amersfoort) **178**
  Piet Hein Tunnel **54**
  Rijksmuseum Twenthe **134–136**
Van Gogh Museum extension
  (Amsterdam) **26**
Van Mourk Vermeulen Architecten bv
  vsb Building **158**
Veldman, Jan 80
Velez, Ani 228
Velsen, Koen van 48, 120, 238
  Library **88**
  Pathé multiplex cinema **236–238**
Vermeulen, Peter 158
Visser, Catherine 174

Vondell Park (Amsterdam) 24
Voorden, Frits van 268
'Vos Maupertus' interior design
   superstore (Groningen) **120**
Vos, Bart van Borselen 120
Vos, Roderick 120
VPRO head office (Hilversum) **72–76**
Vries, Arno de 174
Vries, Auke de 254
Vries, Nathalie de 36, 72, 148, 156, 308,
   316
VSB Building (Utrecht) **158**

Walled-in House (The Hague) 308
Waterpark Neeltje Jans 206
Weeber, Carel **286**
   De Schie penitentiary **278**
   'De Struyck' student housing 284
West 8 Landscape Architects 68, 158, 232
   Binnenrotte Market Square **244**
   Borneo Sporenburg urban development
      46–48
   Schouwburgplein **240**
Wilhelminahof office complex
   (Rotterdam) 268
Winsen, Willem van 194
Witteman, Stefan 76
Wittermans, Hans 268
Woeste Willem child daycare centre
   (Rotterdam) **280**
Woodcock, Andy 142
Woodroffe, Jonathan 162
WOZOCO (Amsterdam) **34–36**

Zaaijer, Aart 160, 308

Zandvoort Circus (amusement centre and
   cinema) **82**
Zeewolde 88
Zielhorst (Amersfoort) 182
Zürich tower (The Hague) 296
Zwart, Lars 238

PHOTOGRAPHS
All photographs are by Anna Neumann
except:
pages 57, 59, 63, 73, 75, 77, 79, 81, 83, 85,
91, 93, 103, 125, 133, 136, 137, 141, 145,
147, 151, 159, 179, 199, 201, 203, 205,
207, 215, 217, 221, 223, 225, 227, 228,
229, 317, 319 by Florian Migsch
page 143 by Scacliola/Brakkee